NEW DIRECTIONS FOR TEACHING AND LEARNING

Marilla D. Svinicki, *University of Texas, Austin*
EDITOR-IN-CHIEF

R. Eugene Rice, *American Association for Higher Education*
CONSULTING EDITOR

Beyond Teaching to Mentoring

Alice G. Reinarz
University of Michigan

Eric R. White
Pennsylvania State University

EDITORS

Number 85, Spring 2001

JOSSEY-BASS
San Francisco

BEYOND TEACHING TO MENTORING
Alice G. Reinarz, Eric R. White (eds.)
New Directions for Teaching and Learning, no. 85
Marilla D. Svinicki, Editor-in-Chief
R. Eugene Rice, Consulting Editor

Microfilm copies of issues and articles are available in 16mm and 35mm,
as well as microfiche in 105mm, through University Microfilms Inc., 300
North Zeeb Road, Ann Arbor, Michigan 48106-1346.

ISSN 0271-0633   ISBN 0-7879-5617-1

NEW DIRECTIONS FOR TEACHING AND LEARNING is part of The Jossey-Bass
Higher and Adult Education Series and is published quarterly by Jossey-
Bass Inc., 350 Sansome Street, San Francisco, California 94104-1342. Peri-
odicals postage paid at San Francisco, California, and at additional mailing
offices. Postmaster: Send address changes to New Directions for Teaching and Learning, Jossey-Bass Inc., 350 Sansome Street, San Francisco,
California 94104-1342.

New Directions for Teaching and Learning is indexed in College Student
Personnel Abstracts, Contents Pages in Education, and Current Index to
Journals in Education (ERIC).

SUBSCRIPTIONS cost $58.00 for individuals and $104.00 for institutions,
agencies, and libraries. Prices subject to change.

EDITORIAL CORRESPONDENCE should be sent to the editor-in-chief, Marilla
D. Svinicki, The Center for Teaching Effectiveness, University of Texas at
Austin, Main Building 2200, Austin, TX 78712-1111.

Cover photograph by Richard Blair/Color & Light © 1990.

www.josseybass.com

Printed in the United States of America on acid-free recycled paper con-
taining 100 percent recovered waste paper, of which at least 20 percent is
postconsumer waste.

CONTENTS

FROM THE SERIES EDITORS

About This Publication. Since 1980, *New Directions for Teaching and Learning* (NDTL) has brought a unique blend of theory, research, and practice to leaders in postsecondary education. NDTL sourcebooks strive not only for solid substance but also for timeliness, compactness, and accessibility.

The series has four goals: to inform readers about current and future directions in teaching and learning in postsecondary education, to illuminate the context that shapes these new directions, to illustrate these new directions through examples from real settings, and to propose ways in which these new directions can be incorporated into still other settings.

This publication reflects our view that teaching deserves respect as a high form of scholarship. We believe that significant scholarship is conducted not only by researchers who report results of empirical investigations but also by practitioners who share disciplined reflections about teaching. Contributors to NDTL approach questions of teaching and learning as seriously as they approach substantive questions in their own disciplines, and they deal not only with pedagogical issues but also with the intellectual and social context in which these issues arise. Authors deal on the one hand with theory and research and on the other with practice, and they translate from research and theory to practice and back again.

About This Volume. This issue focuses on important developments in the area of faculty-student relationships, specifically those involving mentoring. The trend in higher education is to expand the faculty role beyond teaching as defined only as classroom interactions; new definitions recognize that faculty have a more profound affect on students in all areas. The authors of this issue explore what those affects might be and how to maximize their benefits.

MARILLA D. SVINICKI, *editor-in-chief, is director of the Center for Teaching Effectiveness at the University of Texas, Austin.*

R. EUGENE RICE, *consulting editor, is director, Forum on Faculty Roles and Rewards, AAHE.*

Editors' Notes

As a result of the rapid changes affecting higher education, faculty members face continuing challenges to meet their various responsibilities. They must be responsive to evolving technologies, growing costs, and increasing expectations from multiple constituencies. Faculty need to reexamine their interactions with students, both inside and outside the classroom. In the transition to a learning-focused environment—putting the student at the center of the endeavor—instructors will continue to play a major but changing role. Specifically, faculty will need to consider how they mentor students within the context of this shifting educational, social, and technical environment.

During the past few years, the nature of higher education has been studied by a number of committees and commissions. Many reports have called for a reevaluation of the thrust of our efforts, especially in regard to how institutions of higher education relate to students. The question for both administration leaders and individual faculty members is how to respond appropriately in the various institutional and disciplinary cultures.

This volume will examine how faculty might mentor their students. What role will faculty take in preparing students for more active and collaborative learning? How will faculty help students develop the necessary technical, writing, critical thinking, and interpersonal skills? With more consumer-oriented students on campuses, how will faculty help them define their educational goals and make sense of a general education curriculum as part of a total collegiate experience? How will faculty articulate their own passion for their discipline and their scholarship? What should faculty be telling students about how to prepare for careers and lifelong learning?

The audience for this volume is faculty, department heads, and academic administrators. The authors are faculty and administrators representing a variety of disciplines and backgrounds. They will share strategies for mentoring students during a transition to a reshaped higher education environment.

Perhaps the most obvious thread connecting these chapters is the increasing diversity of defining and practicing mentoring among faculty and variations in expectations among current populations of students. Rather than a "how to" book to be read from first to last chapter, instructors and administrators may skip among chapters following the threads of their own particular interests and responsibilities.

Setting the tone for this volume, Diane M. Enerson provides an overview of the philosophy and strategies for teaching through mentoring so that the reader can use the perspectives of all the authors. While the specific possibilities for mentoring are varied among the disciplines and venues described in Chapters Two through Eleven, all faculty can acquire in the first chapter an understanding of current and future opportunities for mentoring inter-actions with students.

When accepting mentoring as a metaphor for teaching, an important shift occurs. Now attention can be paid more to the learner and to the process of learning. What makes this metaphor so compelling is that it comes from the academy. Consequently the understanding and acceptance of such a metaphor can enable us to rethink what teaching is all about, how students relate to instructors, and how they relate to other students. Mentoring carries very little negative baggage with it thus providing a new and unencumbered way to contemplate the teaching and learning endeavor. As Enerson suggests, by using mentoring as a metaphor for teaching, we are provided with the opportunity to reflect on what we do both in the class-room and outside of it. This reflection can lead then to a renewal of spirit and a chance to see just how far the student can outperform the teacher. That all can be comfortable with such an outcome might be the goal of all instruction and serves as the ultimate reward.

In Chapter Two, Edie N. Goldenberg discusses faculty involvement, inside and outside the classroom, in preparing students for their future roles as professionals and as citizens. From her knowledge of programs across the nation, she gives suggestions to help faculty in articulating and promoting a liberal arts education. Organized around a discussion of the essential com-petencies that students must acquire as part of an undergraduate experience, Goldenberg's chapter discusses the rapid changes affecting higher education and their impact on the teaching-mentoring enterprise in the future. She concludes with a specific set of recommendations for faculty—working with colleagues and with students—to optimize the student learning focus in organizing and implementing classroom activities. In these suggestions are the implicit mentoring opportunities unique to the faculty role.

Chapter Three combines the perspectives of a professor and physician, Timothy R. B. Johnson, a student entering medical school, Philip D. Settimi, and a doctoral candidate in public health, Juliet L. Rogers. This uniquely balanced approach provides faculty with a holistic guide to mentoring stu-dents planning to enter the health professions. This chapter describes some challenges particular to students on their way to medical school or other professional or health science schools. In addition, the text offers guidelines to integrate the skills and talents among generalist undergraduate academic advisers, specialized advisers in the health professions, and faculty and com-munity professionals. The resulting team approach to advising, educating, and mentoring prehealth professions students allows optimal opportunities for interactions with undergraduates.

In Chapter Four, Rose M. Marra and Robert N. Pangborn, citing specific opportunities from their own experience, describe best practices for men-toring in the technical disciplines. Designed to enhance student-centered learning, methods to foster peer, faculty, and professional mentoring are detailed. Particularly relevant to technology and engineering programs, mentoring is discussed as an expectation of outcome-based accreditation criteria. The authors describe an ideal mentoring relationship as part of a nonjudgmental environment designed to "reveal the culture of the profession and life beyond the work environment, allow risk-free interchange of aspirations and avocations, disclose the faculty to be truly interested in their students, and foster the nurturing of creative talents and instincts."

With specific information from an undergraduate-fellowships-office model, Mary Gage outlines opportunities to mentor students in developing a global perspective from international study and cultural awareness. Chapter Five offers strategies to expand international experiences for individual students and more broadly for the entire campus population.

Addressing some unique elements of mentoring in communications programs, Chapter Six discusses the dichotomy of teaching in the context of the liberal arts while simultaneously preparing students for the practical elements of the careers that they seek. In order to avoid student confusion in issues where there is tension between professorial and professional views, Jeremy Cohen gives helpful advice to faculty for mentoring strategies that ultimately guide the student from the role of pupil to colleague.

An accomplished teacher and mentor, Brian P. Coppola provides detailed information in Chapter Seven on mentoring opportunities in the sciences. Drawing on models that he has developed at the University of Michigan, Coppola describes the related professional and personal obligations of faculty to guide student development. Mentoring models that he describes include undergraduate research experiences, a structured study group program, a professional development in the sciences capstone course, work with student organizations, and one-on-one interactions with students using Web technology. He closes with a discussion of the philosophical grounding for mentoring by outlining faculty responsibility for teaching through modeling for students of appropriate, thoughtful, forward-looking behaviors.

Reacting to a changing world for living and working, Margaret Scisney-Matlock and John Matlock combine their considerable expertise to discuss some of the unique challenges in mentoring underrepresented students in Chapter Eight. They provide tools particularly useful for faculty whose own education and experience have occurred in institutions with relatively homogeneous populations. This chapter also includes practical applications of strategies for all faculty, regardless of previous experience, in working with all students to help them prepare for an increasingly diverse global society.

Drawing upon significant faculty and administrative experience in Chapter Nine, E. R. Melander provides mentoring strategies particularly for use with undergraduate students in a college of business administration. His approach is holistic, however, and helps faculty understand their changing role. "Faculty long have been representatives of their discipline on campus, concentrating both on expanding pedagogical boundaries and methodologies and on introducing students to the mysteries and marvels of knowledge and its application. Teaching as mentoring shifts faculty attention to questions of how to cause students as individuals to take on responsibilities for their own learning and how to coach them to grow in their capacities for assimilating, developing, applying, and organizing knowledge." This chapter really can apply to faculty in all disciplines.

In Chapter Ten, Timothy L. Killeen provides some strategies to develop curricula that provide special mentoring options delivered in the context of truly interdisciplinary courses. Although first implemented successfully at the University of Michigan, this model, which incorporates faculty, graduate students, and undergraduates from colleges of engineering, science, and natural resources, can be applied at any institution working for effective interdisciplinary instruction. With unique teaching goals and complete utilization of technological support, the Global Change introductory course sequence capitalizes on active learning and effective assessment to raise student enthusiasm for science. Faculty and administrators with hopes that future citizens have appreciation for science and technology will find these mentoring methods particularly attractive.

In Chapter Eleven, Graham B. Spanier, president of The Pennsylvania State University, exhorts faculty to engage in the transformation of teaching and learning that is gaining momentum in the twenty-first century. He argues that the collective faculties of our institutions of higher education today have unprecedented opportunities to influence students through their teaching and mentoring. Responding to rapid change in demographics and student expectations, faculty must redefine the teaching role by "seeking not to provide a fixed education but to inspire and enable lifelong learning." Cognizant of increasing numbers of older, part-time, and underrepresented students, faculty have unique opportunities to "humanize the institution" through mentoring that occurs principally outside the classroom and extends and diversifies the academic experience. Spanier's chapter challenges all in the academic enterprise, especially faculty and administrators, to proactively recognize and adapt to the changing campus culture of the future.

Alice Goodwin Reinarz
Eric R. White
Editors

ALICE GOODWIN REINARZ is currently director of the Academic Advising Center for the College of Literature, Science, and the Arts (LS&A) at the University of Michigan. She is also director of Inteflex, a joint program of the college and the University of Michigan Medical School. As an adjunct associate professor of biology, she currently teaches a class on infectious diseases as part of the LS&A First Year Seminar Program. A recipient of the 1990 Carski Foundation Outstanding Teaching Award for the American Society for Microbiology, she has also published in the areas of undergraduate curriculum reform, and careers for science majors and academic advising.

ERIC R. WHITE *is executive director of the Division of Undergraduate Studies and affiliate assistant professor of education at The Pennsylvania State University. He has been president of the Association of Deans and Directors of University Colleges and Undergraduate Divisions. He has held elected and appointed positions in the National Academic Advising Association and is currently treasurer of that organization. In 1998 the Division of Undergraduate Studies won the Outstanding Institutional Advising Program Award in recognition of innovative and exemplary practice in academic advising.*

1

Fostering open discussions and building community about teaching have often proved problematic within the academy. This chapter discusses how mentoring—when used as a metaphor for teaching—may move us toward solving these problems.

Mentoring as Metaphor: An Opportunity for Innovation and Renewal

Diane M. Enerson

Mentoring is a familiar term that in everyday discourse rarely causes even a momentary flicker of puzzlement. It derives its meaning from the name of a friend to whom Odysseus entrusted his son. Just as Odysseus expected Mentor to counsel and guide Telemachus in order that he might become successful and assume his rightful role in society, we expect mentors—and the mentoring they do—to achieve similar objectives today. The notion that one generation can help the next is certainly not new and seems fundamental. Indeed, it is difficult to imagine how modern civilization would have evolved, or even survived, if each successive generation did not build effectively on the lessons learned in the past.

In recent years, however, mentoring may have become something more—a shibboleth of sorts—ensuring the success of certain groups such as minorities and women while atoning for their lack of success in earlier generations. Interest in and communications about mentoring have grown rapidly during the last few years. That this is the second volume about mentoring in the *New Directions in Teaching and Learning* series during the past decade is certainly reflective of this interest. And even a cursory review of the articles and publications listed in the most recent two or three years of *Higher Education Abstracts* reveals some striking patterns, which may tell us something about the relationship between mentoring and teaching.

One such pattern, and perhaps the most significant, is that mentoring is nearly always associated with one or more highly desirable outcome(s) for those being mentored. Tradition and myth suggest that a mentor will

New Directions for Teaching and Learning, no. 85, Spring 2001 © Jossey-Bass, a Wiley company

give advice that will help those being mentored uncover the tacit assumptions of a discipline, thereby ensuring a level of accomplishment that would not otherwise have been possible. Mentoring becomes a way of revealing the secrets of a profession or discipline for others, a way of showing them not just that it is possible to get a rabbit out of a hat but also how. Mentoring it seems is inherently good.

The second pattern to emerge is a clear shift in common usage from noun to verb. Although "mentoring" is a word that historically has not been listed in most dictionaries and spell checkers as a verb, in everyday discourse we seem to have had little difficulty with this transition. It is a new use of a familiar concept, but its meaning remains clear. Interestingly, when used as a verb it becomes especially noticeable that this is an activity having even less to do with showing others what we can do than with helping them perceive what they can do. The shift from the noun to verb places a clear emphasis on both the process and the learner. Those who have been mentored are expected to succeed; it is how we know they were mentored. Who their mentors are, what those mentors can do, or how they were chosen becomes relatively unimportant.

Such perceptions of mentoring stand in marked contrast to those of teaching, where, historically, considerable emphasis has been placed on what the teacher does rather than on what the student does. Moreover, the outcomes of teaching are not uniformly reported as "good." In fact, it is frequently the custom within discussions about teachers and teaching to expand on the principles and protocol of "good teaching" by contrasting them to those of "bad teaching." This comparative use of good versus bad is rarely the case in discussions or publications about mentoring, where good-bad comparisons—if made at all—are typically external ones, such as between mentoring and teaching.

The chapters in this volume are no exception. Each clearly approaches mentoring as something positive and something that can help to change what happens in our universities and colleges. We learn that those who are mentored will earn more, will become more actively engaged in the subject matter, are more likely to win awards or continue with a course of study, and can more easily make the transition from being passive consumers to being colleagues. But what can our understanding of mentoring tell us about good teaching? Quite possibly, the greatest revelation in a comparison of teaching to mentoring doesn't exist in the details. To duplicate what was done in one case with precision in another will be almost impossible. Often too few details are provided to repeat the experiment. And even if it were possible, it might not always be desirable. What is described as an extraordinary effort in one instructional context may well be viewed as relatively commonplace in another. In mentoring as with teaching, assumptions about the purposes of instruction, use of classroom time, and the nature of appropriate activities can, and probably should, vary greatly (Stodolsky, 1988). What is learned in one instructional context may not apply to the next.

But even if the details of one successful mentoring situation cannot be easily transferred to another, there still may be some important lessons to be learned in the collection of these stories. In their now-classic text, *Metaphors We Live By,* Lakoff and Johnson (1980) begin with the proposal that "metaphor is pervasive in everyday life, not just in language but in thought and action. Our ordinary conceptual system, in terms of which we both think and act, is fundamentally metaphorical in nature" (p. 3). Metaphors, they point out, are a way of understanding one concept by using existing knowledge of another. Thus, when a concept such as teaching becomes metaphorically linked to another, such as mentoring, certain aspects of the first will be rendered more visible. Had a different metaphor been used, different things would be highlighted and hence result in a different behavior and understanding. The effect of any specific metaphor will be at least partially a function of which aspects of a concept are revealed and which are hidden. By so linking mentoring to teaching, we can become more aware of the learner and more likely to act in ways that will have a direct impact on the learner.

Although appeals to focus on the learner are hardly new within the academy (see Dewey, 1938), the metaphors we have used to describe what we do when we teach have not always been ones that cast much light on the learner. Historically, *sage, actor,* and *pedagogue,* among others, have all been used as frequent metaphors for teacher. Unfortunately, all have origins and connotations that focus attention more or less exclusively on what the teacher does, placing little emphasis on the levels of mastery and the accomplishments of the student. With each of these traditional metaphors the evaluative emphasis would therefore be placed on judgments about what the teacher has done. In the past decade an increasing number of voices have been raised in protest. Faculty generally have been compelled by and have identified with Jane Tompkins's self-revelations (1990) about the power and pervasiveness of the performance model in teaching, which she describes as, "putting on a performance whose true goal was not to help the students learn but to perform before them in such a way that they would have a good opinion of me"(p. 654).

Tompkins further argues that because the notion of teacher as performer has traditionally been at the very core of our socialization as scholars, it persists unexamined into the classroom, even when no longer needed or appropriate. The result, Tompkins contends, is that we lose sight of the real goal of the educational process—fostering student learning. Ultimately, however, the ritual of performing persists not simply because it is integral to our socialization as scholars but also because we have kept our role as teacher and the teaching we do hidden from public scrutiny and discourse. Much like sex in Victorian England, teaching becomes "something you weren't suppose to talk about or focus on in any way but you were supposed to be able to do properly when the time came" (Tompkins, 1990, p. 655–656).

That is, in addition to using metaphors for teaching that focus almost exclusively on what the teacher is doing, until very recently it has also been the custom to behave as if teaching was something that should be largely hidden from public view. Indeed, it was less than a decade ago that Lee Shulman confessed his own concern and bewilderment with the degree to which he had been surprised by the paradoxical discovery that teaching was the private part of the scholarly life, while research was the public one.

> What I didn't understand as a new Ph.D. was that I had it backward! We experience isolation not in the stacks but in the classroom. We close the classroom door and experience pedagogical solitude, whereas in our life as scholars, we are members of active communities—communities of conversation, communities of evaluation, communities in which we gather with others in our invisible college to exchange our findings, our methods, and our excuses [Shulman, 1993].

Not surprisingly, as recent appeals to focus on the learner have become increasingly common, persistent, and insistent within the academy, so too have appeals to shed light on our lives as teachers by bringing scholarship and scholarly activity to the classroom (see for example, Schön, 1995; Shulman, 1999; Hutchings and Shulman, 1999). From uncomplicated yet compelling observations that great teachers live forever because they live on in what we do to the more theoretical arguments and position papers that urge faculty to adopt new models and metaphors for what they do when they teach (see for example, Barr and Tagg, 1995; Tompkins, 1990; Shulman, 1999), the message has been clear. Students count. Learning counts. It makes good sense. But have these appeals made a difference? Is there any evidence practice has followed?

Although the escalating nature of such appeals alone might be sufficient to argue that they have had at least a moderate degree of success, in too many instances the voices that are heard probably have not had the effect that was hoped for. There may have been a paradigm shift, but the metaphors we use to guide everyday behavior may not have been helpful. The older ones—such as pedagogue, sage, actor—clearly do not put into the foreground either the learner or what has been learned. The newer ones, however, may seem alien and artificial to many. Teacher as manager (or its frequent partner, student as client) are not metaphors that ring true for most faculty. Hence, they can't be useful. For a metaphor to be effective we must have some knowledge of the metaphor being applied; in fact, the more complete our knowledge the better. Few faculty, however, would have sufficient knowledge of the concepts of managing, facilitating, or even coaching for these newly applied metaphors to shed any new light on their understanding of teaching. Only a few among us can coach, somewhat more can facilitate, and teacher as manager seems even harder to apply. These metaphors ask us to apply remote and alien concepts; they are unhelpful and thus easy to dismiss.

But the metaphor of teacher as mentor seems harder to dismiss. It presents an image and concept that originates from within the academy, not from outside. We are all familiar with what it means to be mentored. We have all been mentored and most of us believe we have mentored others. It is an integral part of our culture of the academy. Thus the metaphor of teaching as mentoring is an invitation to improve by looking within ourselves for other ways of doing business. Especially when used as a verb it becomes both familiar and new. It asks not that we adopt new rituals but that we look for different arrangements for the existing ones. It is a compelling metaphor that derives its greatest strength from our shared cultural assumptions of what it means to be mentored. And because it comes from within, it highlights not just what teachers must do but also the context and the role institutions must play to ensure that mentoring occurs. That is, it highlights what the teachers must do while also highlighting the large context and community within which they do it.

That the context for learning is implicated by the word mentoring seems important. Typically, institutional practices have not always been ones that made it easy to focus on the learner. For example, reviews and evaluations of teaching in many institutions focus nearly exclusively on what the teacher does, not on what the students do. The reasons seem obvious. First, it is far simpler to count a few easily observable behaviors of an individual teacher than to complete the complex inferential calculus required to account for the impact of those behaviors on the learning of not just one, or even twenty, but often hundreds of students. But if the focus in our evaluation of teaching is shifted to what is learned, the questions that we ask—and the unit of our analyses—must shift as well. How, for example, are faculty rewarded for their achievements as teachers? Is the sequence of educational experiences structured in such a way that students are socialized to the importance of their own learning? In what ways do institutional policies facilitate student success? In what ways do they celebrate it? In what ways do they impede it?

Questions that will help us evaluate those successes of our teaching will be asked not just of individuals, but also at the departmental, college, and institutional levels as well. Successful mentoring—much like teaching—will be bound by the constraints imposed by the limitations and strengths of individuals and broader instructional context involved.

Ultimately, then, we learn the most from using mentoring as a metaphor for teaching if we place the greatest emphasis not just on what is learned by virtue of a single classroom experience but on what is learned and accomplished by virtue of an individual's total experience.

This point is similar to and a logical extension of the earlier proposal that we "rethink mentoring in higher education, to construct a more holistic and organic model, to place it squarely in the context of the educational culture, and to conform the disconnection between individual and institutional goals" (Wunsch, 1994, p. 10). Our goals, however, are somewhat different. Where Wunsch's was an appeal to integrate mentoring programs into the organizational structure of institutions, the present one is a broader and less deliberately prescriptive one; namely that we use our understanding of mentoring and its role within the academy as an opportunity for renewal and change, and that we use it as a way to reflect on questions that get to the very core of our daily activities in the classroom and in larger institutional contexts in which those classrooms are situated. Quite clearly, part of the intrinsic appeal and ultimate power of the teaching as mentoring metaphor is that it clearly provides an opportunity for individual teachers as well as institutions to reflect on or examine the contexts they provide for learning.

Obviously, not all students will want or benefit from a one-on-one personal relationship with each teacher they encounter. But when the larger institutional context is implicated, we can allow for that. The kind of nurturing and attention to individual needs and potential that mentoring implies requires a setting where student achievement is celebrated publicly. And it also implies that to do this effectively requires a context where faculty rewards for teaching are sources of public celebration and everyday discourse as well. Thus, like the various recent appeals to foster a broader definition of scholarship and scholarly teaching (for example, Boyer, 1990; Cross, 1990; Hutchings and Shulman, 1999; Shulman, 1999), the appeal for mentoring as a metaphor for teaching is an internal call for renewal of change. Leonardo da Vinci once observed that it is a poor teacher whose students do not exceed him. Using mentoring as a metaphor for teaching, in time, can move us closer to that ideal.

References

Barr, R. B., and Tagg, J. "From Teaching to Learning—A Paradigm for Undergraduate Education." *Change,* Nov./Dec. 1995, 27(6), 12–25.

Boyer, E. L. *Campus Life: In Search of Community.* Princeton, N.J.: The Carnegie Foundation for the Advancement of Teaching, 1990.

Cross, K. P. "Teachers as Scholars." *AAHE Bulletin,* December 1990, 43(4), 3–5.

Dewey, J. *Experience and Education.* New York: Macmillan, 1938.

Hutchings, P., and Shulman, L. S. "The Scholarship of Teaching." *Change,* Sept./Oct. 1999, 31(5), 11–15.

Lakoff, G., and Johnson, M. *Metaphors We Live By.* Chicago: University of Chicago Press, 1980.

Schön, D. "The New Scholarship Requires a New Epistemology: Knowing in Action" *Change,* Nov./Dec. 1995, 27(6), 26–34.

Shulman, L. S. "Displaying Teaching to a Community of Peers." Speech Presented at the American Association for Higher Education National Conference, Stanford University, January 1993.

Shulman, L. S. "Taking Learning Seriously." *Change,* July/Aug. 1999, 31(4), 11–17.

Stodolsky, S. S. *The Subject Matters: Classroom Activity in Math and Social Studies.* Chicago and London: The University of Chicago Press, 1988.

Tompkins, J. "Pedagogy of the Distressed." *College English* 52.6 (1990), 653–660.
Wunsch, M. A. "New Directions for Mentoring: An Organizational Development Perspective." In Wunsch, M. A. (ed.). *Mentoring Revisited: Making an Impact on Individuals and Institutions,* New Directions for Teaching and Learning, no. 57. San Francisco: Jossey-Bass, 1994.

DIANE M. ENERSON is director of the Center for Excellence in Learning and Teaching, assistant professor of liberal arts, and affiliate assistant professor of educational psychology at Penn State University.

2

This chapter focuses on what liberal arts students should learn, given the future they face, and how educational experiences can provide opportunities for that learning to take place. Mentoring is an important means by which a faculty member can promote effective learning.

Teaching Key Competencies in Liberal Arts Education

Edie N. Goldenberg

What do liberal arts students need to learn? That question has captured the time and energy of academics and others for more than a century, and there is no single generally accepted answer in sight. Nor should there be. One's answer depends on one's view of what a liberal arts education is meant to achieve and one's guess about what life for today's students will be like in the coming decades. In this chapter, I reflect upon my experience as dean for nine years of a large liberal arts college engaged in seriously rethinking undergraduate education within an even larger research university. First, I address three questions:

1. Why study the liberal arts?
2. What challenges will our students face in the future?
3. What do those challenges imply for today's educational programs in the liberal arts?

Then I conclude with some thoughts as I return to the faculty and become personally reinvolved in the world of classroom teaching.

Why Study the Liberal Arts?

A liberal arts education is a meaningful introduction to fundamental questions, ideas, and methods in several fields of inquiry and an intensive introduction to at least one field, the major. In order to provide sufficient breadth, the several fields normally include exposure to the humanities, sciences, and social sciences. A liberal arts degree does *not* signify training for employment in any immediate sense, even as it is widely recognized as an excellent foundation for a multitude of job opportunities and for graduate and professional study.

More than ever before, a liberal arts education is of special value today. A successful liberal arts experience can be a source of personal satisfaction for students throughout their lives. It has staying power beyond the short half-life of technical training because it introduces students to fundamental issues as they have been explored by others through the ages. A liberal arts major should provide exposure to ideas, feelings, and situations that are common to human experience and to the ways that respected minds and revered hearts have dealt with them. Through the mentoring process, faculty in the liberal arts deepen this exposure and help students relate it to their own futures.

The goals of a liberal arts education are to provide students with a solid foundation for problem solving; to help them understand others and interact effectively with them; to help students examine their own assumptions and avoid being taken in by specious argument; to help students feel connected with others who have dealt with similar feelings or situations or problems; to open students' eyes and minds to the fascinations of other cultures and experiences; to provide a deeper sense of self and citizenship, and to develop valued employees, responsible citizens, and effective leaders. Inside and outside the classroom, liberal arts students should learn *how* to learn and develop a zest for learning that will last them a lifetime.

Liberal arts students study what physicists or philosophers or poets or psychologists think about, how they go about their deliberations, and how they decide what they do and don't know. Students who are fortunate enough to study with active scholars learn how to learn from those who are lifetime experts at learning. In this way, students are exposed to what others regard as questions worth asking and goals worth pursuing. The faculty mentor is a role model and guide. In an ideal liberal arts setting, students learn to consider assertions critically, to decide what evidence deserves attention and what can be dismissed, and to distinguish careful arguments from sloppy ones. In my view, this is the heart of a liberal arts education: developing critical thinking skills and the ability to apply them to observations, arguments, and conclusions, thereby becoming less bound by one's own prejudices and rationalizations. Provided by the teacher and mentor, a quality liberal arts education helps students develop a proper balance between openness to new ideas and a healthy skepticism of those same ideas, a balance that permits knowledge to advance today and to continue to advance tomorrow.

Students learn in the classroom, of course, but they also can learn a great deal in less-formal settings from faculty and other mentors. The undergraduate research experience provides an ideal opportunity for research-oriented faculty to become effective mentors. The faculty member is comfortable in research situations; the student benefits from individualized coaching on everything from problem definition to data gathering to analysis to the ethical dilemmas in research. Research experiences work most powerfully when a faculty member and a student apprentice interact frequently and easily enough for the relationship to broaden to include academic advising and career counseling.

Achieving for the student a desirable blend of solid grounding in a field of study and broad exposure to multiple fields occupies academics as we design and redesign college curricula and create new learning experiences outside the classroom. Our tinkering never stops because students' needs change over time and because in their undergraduate years students cannot possibly learn all, or even most, of what they will need to know. Of course students need to learn computational, observational, and communication skills, but skills are not enough. With skills, they may be well trained, but to be well educated, they need to know *how* to continue learning long after they leave campus, and most of their later learning will occur outside of formal classroom settings.

Whether we achieve our ideals in liberal arts education is an empirical question that remains largely unanswered. For institutions of learning, universities are shockingly remiss when it comes to careful study of the effectiveness of their own educational programs. And even those general research findings that provide important insights into students' learning are often ignored. Nonetheless, periodic reexamination of our ideals is a worthwhile exercise in that it forces faculty to break out of habit, try to forecast as well as we can what our students will face in their futures, and rethink and occasionally redesign the learning environments we offer.

What faculty *do* spend a great deal of time and effort on is periodic debate over the appropriate content of course requirements. Much of the controversy over appropriate curricular content in the liberal arts swirls around departments of literature and history. Some people apparently include only the humanities and the social sciences in their definitions of the liberal arts. Mathematics and science are, have been, and continue to be important parts of a liberal arts education. Universities began recognizing this by the mid-1800s when presidents added science to literary departments. The "newcomers" to the liberal arts are not the sciences but rather fine arts, music, and the social sciences (Bordin, 1967; Peckham, 1967). If students are to be educated in a broad range of the liberal arts, we need to encourage nonscience majors to learn some science. We also need to relax the rigidity of some of our science concentrations to allow students to study the humanities and social sciences and to participate in the creative arts and overseas study.

What Will the Future Hold for Our Students?

We can observe features of U.S. society today that carry implications for how we educate our undergraduates, and we can make some informed guesses about the future. Today is a time of complex problems and dazzlingly rapid change. On the one hand, complexity encourages more and more special-ization—more detailed study of smaller and smaller parts of problems. On the other hand, complexity means that understanding and solving problems often require broader knowledge than any single person commands. That is why teamwork has become so highly valued in the workplace. Real prob-lems are multifaceted. They do not sort themselves neatly into disciplinary boxes. They are seldom exclusively political or ethical or economic or tech-nical, but often all of the above. Problem solvers who are too specialized cannot be effective. They need to understand links across fields and they need to be able to cooperate with others who bring needed complementary expertise to the problem-solving mix.

Complexity drives the need for well-educated workers. Fewer and fewer jobs with reasonable wages can be performed adequately by people who lack reading, writing, arithmetic, reasoning, and communication skills. For the first time in history, a majority of new jobs in the United States require postsecondary education (Johnston and Packer, 1987). People will change jobs and occupations more frequently than before, making broad education and widely applicable skills even more important to a student's future.

Moreover, employees are working with a more diverse set of cowork-ers than in the past. Only 15 percent of new entrants to the labor force over the 1990s were native white males, as compared to 47 percent in 1987 (Johnston and Packer, 1987). Effectiveness in the workplace today requires communicating clearly and interacting with a demographically diverse set of coworkers. That will become even more important in the future.

The complexity of public problems also drives the need for a better-educated voting public. Many policy domains such as national defense, the economy, pollution, or public health are highly technical. Arguments about choices cite scientific evidence at a time when national studies (Fox, 1999) express alarm at the shortages of science and math teachers and the poor preparation of U.S. students in science. Science and math literacy, too, will become more and more important over time.

In this context, citizens and leaders need education that is both broad and deep. The problems at the top of our agenda change quickly. Many we hear about now—for example, AIDS, global warming, U.S. policy toward a united Germany—were not even on most agendas fifteen years ago. Our leaders should be well prepared to address a wide variety of problems, including new ones as they emerge, and to recognize and understand their interconnectedness. Effective leaders must also be capable of building coali-tions and motivating people of widely different backgrounds and experi-ences. This requires breadth and problem-solving skills, preparation for a wide variety of roles and situations, and understanding of different approaches and perspectives.

With the help of the faculty mentor, students need to develop their individual skills and much more. They also need to know how to identify which questions are worth asking, which problems can be solved with current tools and approaches, which goals are worth pursuing. We look to our citizens and leaders to choose goals wisely. We expect our leaders to motivate other individuals and organizations to behave in ways that further those goals, and to do so in the midst of constraints and opportunities that constantly impinge on the individuals and organizations they lead.

Effective individuals learn to operate through large-scale, complex institutions that are a fact of life in business, government, the courts, the media, hospitals, universities, and even U.S. charitable foundations. As Max Weber (1947) observed, these inventions of the twentieth century are superb vehicles for efficiently coordinating the efforts of many people as they pursue organizational goals. Bureaucracies have their advantages but they can also hamper adaptability, creativity, individuality, and renewal. Once set, bureaucratic rules can take on lives of their own, sometimes working mindlessly to produce undesirable and unintended results. Our students need to learn to see the whole and not only the efficiently operating parts. To succeed in most walks of life, they will need the skills to move large organizations in positive directions. That is no small task. As he thought about the ingredients necessary for effective leadership, John Gardner (1988) cited the ability to work with and through large complex organized institutions as the "single most important feature of 20th century leadership." Surely that will remain a reality in the twenty-first century as well. An education well-grounded in the liberal arts is one way for students to begin to acquire the breadth of knowledge necessary to be effective in large institutions.

Given the dizzying pace of change, the complexity of problems, the growing diversity of the population, and the reality of large organizations, academics need to think carefully once again about the central elements of a liberal arts education.

What Are Key Competencies in the Liberal Arts Today?

The literature on student learning dates back to the nineteenth century. The evidence is compelling that students learn more when they are engaged and involved, they learn more when they cooperate with each other, and the quality of teaching affects what students learn (Astin, 1993; Pascarella and Terenzini, 1991; Johnson, Johnson, and Smith, 1991). Yet faculty members are often slow to adjust their classroom approaches and routines and may overlook out-of-class mentoring opportunities. The time is ripe to pay more attention to the evidence we have on student learning—to design courses that actively involve students in their own learning and to design cooperative learning experiences. The reengagement of senior faculty in first- and second-year seminars is a positive step, especially if these seminars stimulate active in-class participation and significant self-directed (with faculty guidance) student projects. Undergraduate research experiences are also wonderful opportunities for student engagement in original discovery and cooperative learning.

At the University of Michigan we have found research experiences to be especially valuable in the sophomore year and additionally valuable to upper-class undergraduate and graduate mentors of the sophomore researchers (Nagda and others, 1998). The focus on cooperative problem solving in calculus and chemistry instruction is yet another positive step (Ewing, 1999; Ege, Coppola, and Lawton, 1997; Coppola, Ege, and Lawton, 1997). In the humanities and the social sciences, exposure to writings by and about people from other cultures helps students understand different perspectives and practices. There is something quite powerful in having students of different backgrounds engage each other in structured conversations around topics that bring out their different perspectives. The dialogue groups at Michigan are wonderful vehicles for fostering constructive conversations (Schoem, Frankel, Zuniga, and Lewis, 1993). These are all examples of faculty-led educational efforts in the liberal arts that take advantage of what we know about student learning and what we believe are important societal trends as we help students build competencies that will be important all though their lives. But even more needs to be done.

Another widely accepted finding about student learning is that students learn more when their extracurricular activities reinforce what they study in their classes (Astin, 1993). Yet a recent report of a survey of three hundred colleges and universities concludes that an "invisible wall separates academic life from the nonacademic side of college, a division reinforced on many campuses by separate administrative structures that seldom intersect" (Gaff, 1991, p. 129). As university presidents have become personally committed to improving undergraduate education and stemming the flow of criticism of the academy, the matter of how we teach and how students learn has been elevated to a level on campus that can bring classroom and non-classroom activity together. The growth of living-learning programs on many campuses is a testament to that, as are the growth in research opportunities for undergraduates on and off campus and the growth in community service as part of in-class experiences. Administrators and faculty members can work together to enhance the mentoring options available to undergraduates.

Improvements are possible and clearly necessary in the way we approach a liberal arts education, but how are we to achieve them? One observer suggested that "the progress of an institution . . . will be directly proportional to the death rate of the faculty" (Rudolph, 1977, p. 17), but surely that is excessively cynical. Clark Kerr (1982) noted that the two great periods of change in U.S. higher education—the 1870s and the 1960s— were both periods of rapid enrollment growth and addition of new faculty and programs. Now we are faced with the challenge of changing in desirable ways during an extended period of no or slow growth.

The obvious place to start is with the faculty. Liberal arts education today is well served by a faculty active in research. Who can better communicate the ways to learn and the commitment to learn for life than a faculty comprising people who chose to pursue careers of learning? They are living, breathing models of learning for life. When students work closely with faculty who are active in research, the students can experience learning with its highs and lows, from tedious attention to detail to the excitement of a new insight. They can see how an expert works with objects or people or experiments or texts. They can learn a great deal about the importance of integrity in learning and sharing what one learns with others. This is a not a unidirectional benefit. Research-active faculty members gain too from their exposure to undergraduates who ask for simple explanations, who ask naive questions about why particular questions are important, and who remind senior faculty members of the thrill that comes to a beginner who experiences the "aha" of discovery and understanding. Perhaps that is why over 90 percent of the Michigan faculty who have volunteered to work with first- or second-year students in research volunteer again the following year.

Thoughts to Guide My Reentry as an Undergraduate Teacher and Mentor

During my nine years as dean, I stepped out of a classroom teaching role in political science and public policy into what became my own mid-career liberal arts education with outstanding faculty in the humanities, sciences, and social sciences. My perspective will never be the same. As I reenter my professorial role and the classroom, I do so differently than before. These are a few of the lessons I have learned and the steps I now remind myself to take.

- Tell students why I think a question is important and show them how I approach answering it, giving them a sense of the blind alleys of inquiry as well as the neatness and logic of the solution. Students benefit from learning what we do and how we think even if they have no inclination to become professional academics themselves.
- Design learning opportunities that encourage undergraduates to work with each other and learn from each other.
- Construct some examples from other fields, with the help of my colleagues, and compare how similar questions are asked and answered in my field with how they are asked and answered in others.
- Call on a colleague in another department or a professional school to come talk with undergraduates about why learning in my field is important, and (of course) reciprocate if asked.
- Work closely with a few undergraduate students on my research or on designing class assignments or a course, and allow these experiences to develop into broader advising and mentoring relationships.

- Find ways for more senior students to be trained to mentor first- and second-year students. This benefits both the mentors and those being mentored.
- Ask the residence halls, the film society, or student clubs to plan programs that complement the topics covered in my course.
- Work with colleagues to design careful evaluations of teaching innovations.
- Enjoy my students. Let them experience the joy of discovery and remind me of just how exciting it was for me when I was just a beginner.

The liberal arts have never been more important than they are now in this age of information and rapid change. In their classrooms, their laboratories, and their lives, faculty mentors are in a wonderful position to help students become well educated and better prepared for their futures. Research-active faculty from all over the university can make a significant difference if they are willing to engage undergraduate students in actively creative endeavors. Working with students in this way brings joy to the learning experience for students and faculty too.

References

Astin, A. W. *What Matters in College? Four Critical Years Revisited.* San Francisco: Jossey-Bass, 1993.

Bordin, R. *The University of Michigan: A Pictorial History.* Ann Arbor: The University of Michigan Press, 1967.

Coppola, B. P., Ege, S. N., and Lawton, R. G. "The University of Michigan Undergraduate Chemistry Curriculum.2. Instructional Strategies and Assessment." *Journal of Chemical Education,* 1997, *74,* 84–94.

Ege, S. N., Coppola, B. P., and Lawton, R. G. "The University of Michigan Undergraduate Chemistry Curriculum.1. Philosophy, Curriculum, and the Nature of Change." *Journal of Chemical Education,* 1997, *74,* 74–83.

Ewing, J. (ed.). *Towards Excellence: Leading a Doctoral Mathematics Department in the 21st Century.* Providence, R.I.: American Mathematical Society Task Force on Excellence, 1999.

Fox, M. A. (chair). *Transforming Undergraduate Education in Science, Mathematics, Engineering, and Technology.* Committee on Undergraduate Science Education, National Research Council, Washington, D.C., 1999.

Gaff, J. *New Life for the College Curriculum: Assessing Achievements and Furthering Progress in the Reform of General Education.* San Francisco: Jossey-Bass, 1991.

Gardner, J. W. *The Changing Nature of Leadership.* Leadership Papers/11, July 1988, 3–24.

Johnson, D. W., Johnson, P. T., and Smith, K. A. *Cooperative Learning,* ASHE-ERIC Higher Education Report No. 4. Washington, D.C.: Association for the Study of Higher Education and The George Washington University, 1991.

Johnston, W. B., and Packer, A. H. *Workforce 2000: Work and Workers for the 21st Century.* Indianapolis: Hudson Institute, 1987.

Kerr, C. "Postscript 1982: The Uses of the University Two Decades Later." *Change,* Sept./Oct. 1982, *14,* 23–31.

Nagda, B. A., Gregerman, S. R., Jonides, J., von Hippel, W., and Lerner, J. S., "Undergraduate Student-Faculty Research Partnerships Affect Student Retention." *The Review of Higher Education,* Fall 1998, 22(1), 55–72.

Pascarella, E. T., and Terenzini, P. T. *How College Affects Students: Findings and Insights from Twenty Years of Research.* San Francisco: Jossey-Bass, 1991.

Peckham, H. *The Making of the University of Michigan, 1817–1967.* Ann Arbor: The University of Michigan Press, 1967.

Rudolph, F. "Frames of Reference." *Curriculum: A History of the Undergraduate Course of Study Since 1636.* San Francisco: Jossey-Bass, 1977, 1–24.

Schoem, D., Frankel, L., Zuniga, X., and Lewis, E. A. *Multicultural Teaching in the University.* Westport, Conn.: Praeger, 1993.

Weber, M. *Theory of Economic and Social Organization.* (A. M. Henderson and T. Parsons, trans.). Glencoe, Ill.: Free Press, 1947.

Edie N. Goldenberg is professor of political science and public policy at the University of Michigan in Ann Arbor. She was dean of the College of Literature, Science and the Arts at Michigan from 1989 through 1998.

3

With specific ideas drawing from the diverse perspectives of its authors, this chapter describes opportunities that extend beyond advising to mentoring for those undergraduates who aspire to careers in the health professions. Although issues in the health sciences mirror those in education in general, the mentoring network described here utilizes individuals who can provide unique insights for students interested in the health professions.

Mentoring for the Health Professions

Timothy R. B. Johnson, Philip D. Settimi, and Juliet L. Rogers

In 1977, John Bruhn wrote "[p]remedicine and medicine are worlds apart. . . . There is an acute need to revise premedical advising to better meet the needs of students. Medical schools should share the responsibility and initiatives in creating a system whereby career choices are made by positive actions" (Bruhn, 1977, p. 678). Despite Bruhn's plea, we believe there has been no systematic improvement or change in the premedical advising process, much less for those with nonmedical prehealth interests, in the last twenty-five years. Opportunities abound for improvements in appropriate-career selection, preprofessional preparation, and facilitation and improvement of the application process for potential premedical and other prehealth students. We hope the current interest in mentorship can focus on neglected issues and lead to a more satisfying process for individuals as well as more appropriate societal distribution of new, intelligent service providers.

College advisers, in addition to traditional academic advising, have the opportunity to improve and enrich prehealth students' growth by also becoming mentors, encouraging and enabling students to identify other mentors, and working to develop an effective and informed mentor network. Mentoring is a teaching opportunity to guide students as they explore their nonacademic interests and their values. Mentors with insights about the joys and challenges in health professions are well positioned to help students evaluate their choices and understand the far-reaching consequences of those choices. The mentor does not give all the answers but instead helps students begin to pose all the questions.

NEW DIRECTIONS FOR TEACHING AND LEARNING, no. 85, Spring 2001   © Jossey-Bass, a Wiley company

Career Selection

There is an increasing variety of health professions and health-related careers available to students. Many undergraduate students begin as premedical students not realizing that other satisfying careers are available or that these other careers might be either preferable from a personal point of view or more realistically attainable. Ensuring that students have adequate exposure to opportunities in nursing, social work, public health, and related health professions (physical therapy, respiratory therapy, occupational therapy, music and dance therapy) is increasingly appropriate given the fierce premedical competition. Linked with this is the importance of reality testing for those students for whom medical school is not a viable option. Early encouragement of these students includes presenting them with a broad potential list of opportunities. Challenges will remain in reaching those students who do not hear the advice given or fail to use existing advising services (Trevino, Fuentes, and Bruhn, 1977).

Roles for the Mentor

Mentors should be readily accessible to observe the decision-making process and offer suggestions to guide it. The best mentors will never attempt to make decisions for the student. Ideally a mentor-student relationship can be founded on similar professional, academic, or community interests. It can be of assistance, though not necessary, for mentors to be well-known in their community and to be current with the job-search or grad-school-research process. It may only be necessary for students to meet with their mentors two to four times annually. While that may match the number of visits to the Undergraduate Advising Office, the quality of the meeting may be higher given a more relaxed, focused atmosphere. In any case, the simple fact that the mentor does not have to spend time with many other students or be concerned with some academic issues should allow for a more personal relationship to develop.

After identifying a viable mentor, the student should be aware that the mentor's expertise is not described by which science classes are most difficult or how many to schedule in a semester. That is a job for the general prehealth adviser. Instead, a mentor will be able to listen to a student's thoughts, observe his or her activities outside of school, and offer suggestions about how to identify additional opportunities and long-term goals. For example, while recommending a standard hospital internship, a mentor might observe a student's interest in technology and identify biotechnology or bioengineering opportunities. A prehealth student might be advised to intern with a health economist or study health law.

It has been suggested that dual processes should be used, those of academic advising and separate career and professional counseling by either a preprofessional committee or an office of career planning and placement

(Bruhn, 1977; Trevino, Fuentes, and Bruhn, 1977; Elam, Lenhoff, and Johnson, 1997). We believe local history and culture will determine institutional practice but that the issues and concerns we discuss should be systemically recognized and addressed.

An important role of the mentor is helping students develop an appropriate record not only academically but of preprofessional activities and community service. This will inevitably play a role in defining the students' career goals. Another important piece early on is assuming that the students are quite clear that they understand what medicine is, what public health is, and what the possible internships are. A variety of experiences are critical to allow students to explore opportunities and to pick the appropriate career paths. Once the appropriate and realistic career choice with viable and interesting alternative options is made, then the next step is easier: achievement of all the curricular, extracurricular, and community service activities that will maximize the student's candidacy.

Curriculum or Classes and Grades

The mentor should be generally aware of the curricular requirements and performance standards for acceptance to medical school and where more specific, reliable information can be obtained. The fact that most medical admission committees emphasize GPA and MCAT scores over noncognitive or community service achievements is clear (Trevino, Fuentes, and Bruhn, 1977; Hesser, Cregler, and Lewis, 1998). It is also clear that expectations from other health-professional schools may be less explicit and these should be sought from the school themselves.

Medical school admission officers and clinical faculty are also demonstrably interested in students with exposure to humanities and social sciences (Elam, Lenhoff, and Johnson, 1997; Imperato, 1997; Stimmel, Smith, and Kase, 1995). The fact that except for in biochemistry there is no benefit from electing advanced science courses that will reappear in the medical curriculum (Caplan, Kreiter, and Albanese, 1996) should lead to a broad curricular experience. Mentors could participate in and encourage this shift in concentration emphasis.

Opportunities for premedical, career-focused academic classes (Gerbens, Stid, and Foulds, 1998), seminars (Abdelman, Bryon, and Davidson, 1995), and hospital or premedical student internships (Alexander, Nevins, Lyon, Thayer, and Yere, 1983; Alexander, Lyon, Nevins, Yere, and Thayer, 1992) are all described and have been effective in helping students identify appropriate careers, and yet these competitive programs may be difficult to locate unless mentors remain continually vigilant for such opportunities. Specific opportunities for minority students after successful completion of summer academic enrichment programs have shown the programs' benefits (Hesser, Cregler, and Lewis, 1998; Bruhn, Fuentes, Trevino, and Williams, 1976).

Application

After a career has been selected, and the appropriate internships, academic prerequisites, and personal growth have been identified, the application process needs attention. "Packaging" the applicant and ensuring appropriate "etiquette" during the application or admission process can maximize the candidate's success. The preprofessional committee or the professional counseling office often collects materials and makes summary recommendations that carry great weight. Mentors and institutions need to understand that academic applications are different from job applications; recommendations, dossiers, and evaluations should follow academic expectations. Students need advice about letters of recommendation. Too often these are requested of faculty with no knowledge of the values and perspective of medical or graduate program admission committees, even if they do have adequate knowledge of the students. Such letters often open with the fact that the student took their class and got a fine grade, and then go on to describe their class syllabus, their teaching goals, or their grading methods. Mentors should help students find and select recommendors and assist with the application package.

Unsuccessful applicants to medical school can and should have mentoring opportunities, optimally initiated before the rejection occurs, so they can quickly pursue attractive available options (Becker, Katatsky, and Seidel, 1973). Ideally, these students should have received adequate early counseling so that those likely to be admitted to medical school can reassess and reapply. Those less likely to achieve acceptance should have an alternative in place, which they actively pursue while applying to professional school. This prevents delay following rejection and permits early and satisfied selection of the predetermined alternative.

Beyond the Medical School Option

With appropriate academic and career advising, quality mentoring, and enlightening experiential learning opportunities, a considerable number of premedical undergraduates discover that medical school may not be the best fit for their interests or lifestyle goals. This is not where the advising relationship ends. Rather, it is where the greatest opportunity exists for the relationship to flourish. A plethora of career, graduate school, and employment opportunities exist for those students interested in health-science fields such as public health, health promotion, environmental health, gerontology, health management, movement science, midwifery, nursing, dental hygiene, and occupational and physical therapy.

For some students, these careers are the focus from the beginning and individualized, prehealth science advising should be offered to them in the first year. Other students have no exposure to and little knowledge of these areas of study and are introduced to them only after deciding that medical school is not for them or is out of reach for the time being. In either case, high-quality advice regarding the best course of study for prehealth science students, internship and career opportunities, professional societies, and accredited graduate school programs is often unavailable to these students. One reason for this is because the plans of study must be developed for each student based on the health-science area of interest. Graduate programs in occupational health have preparation and admission requirements that differ greatly from those of graduate programs in health-services management. Nonetheless, at the undergraduate level, students with very different interests and goals are often limited to the same academic advising options— those of the prehealth science advisers.

Some universities are trying to address this and related issues by offering one-hour workshops that are designed to introduce first- and second-year students to a range of careers that may be of interest to those who are considering medical and nursing fields. The most helpful of these workshops will often feature panels of established professionals representing different interest areas and panelists who can articulate to students the many different paths (as opposed to set curricula) that students may choose at the undergraduate level if admission to graduate school is the end goal. Peer advising (another form of mentoring) that matches prehealth undergraduates with graduate students who are pursuing studies in the area of interest are often very helpful, especially at smaller schools where advisers with personal experience with health-science graduate programs may be in short supply.

Innovative Opportunities for Mentorship

It may not be until the third or fourth years of undergraduate study that some students discover their areas of interest. For these students, it is often difficult to complete their degrees in the regular time frame if a change in area of concentration or major course requirements is introduced as a result of their change in direction. Introducing students to the myriad of choices in the health-science professions at early stages in their undergraduate careers is one way to reduce the likelihood that this will happen for students interested in prehealth. The previous section identified career-planning workshops as one way to inform students of their options. Another way is to take the workshops to them, meeting them wherever they may be at that time. This can be achieved easily through curricular and experiential integration of "less traditional" health-science topics into the traditional health-science introductory courses. Undergraduate teachers should be encouraged to provide such mentorship by faculty administration and working with offices that also provide resources for successful implementation.

Take, for example, introductory biology. At larger universities, the introductory biology course for prehealth and science students may enroll five hundred students or more each term. Little time would be taken away, and much value would be added to the students' experience, if parts of one or several lectures included examples of how the theories or experiments related to the day's subject matter could be applied or expanded to fields of study with which students are less familiar. Instead of a discussion on how the physician or biologist would use the information, perhaps the students could be offered perspectives on the value of the information for the environmental health researcher or the dietician. To take this example further, consider the number of students who may be interested in hearing how the findings resulting from the biologist's experiment might help strengthen the argument of the women's health advocate or the health-policy analyst. The opportunities for this type of integration may not exist in each class session, but would certainly fit in a few over the course of the term.

Beyond health-science preparatory courses, many opportunities exist in social science and humanities curricula to introduce students to different fields of health-science study. Many women's-studies programs now feature courses in women's and reproductive health, health advocacy and activism, and the biology of women's cancers. English courses have been developed that emphasize the skills required for science and technical writing; others emphasize the power of the narrative for those with chronic health conditions. Sociology, American culture, and other social science and humanities departments increasingly are offering opportunities for students to gain exposure to lesser-known careers through experiential learning courses and community service projects. Experiential learning offers students on-the-job training, an environment in which to test their knowledge and apply their skills, and the opportunity to make valuable connections with potential future employers and reference writers.

Traditionally, established programs in experiential learning for pre-health science students were limited to "shadowing" or lab assistantships. Though both present a valuable opportunity for the aspiring doctor or medical researcher, they offer little to students who are interested in health-career options other than medical or research fields. Resources should now be directed to the development of complementary programs to better serve the interests of pre–public health students, while expanding the scope of the learning opportunities for premedical students. These programs should include experiential learning opportunities in government and private health advocacy and health-policy research agencies, schools, correctional facilities, community projects and social service programs, and other charities or nonprofits. Pre–public and allied-health students will gain valuable exposure to many career paths, premedical students will learn the importance of community health efforts in achieving wellness and preventing disease, and the community will benefit from the energy, enthusiasm, and project support of all students involved.

Redesigning the Advisory or Mentor Network

In order to fulfill the complete support role for today's prehealth students, colleges and universities should consider emphasizing a coordinated and complementary advising system based on the use of traditional academic advisers and novel community- or university-affiliated mentors.

Under the traditional system of undergraduate advising for premedical students, now more broadly defined as prehealth students, a subset of the much larger advisory network supports an oftentimes unwieldy volume of students. With such a large percentage of undergraduates seeking prehealth advising, at many universities waiting times for advisers can be lengthy. In addition, appointments can be brief, impersonal, and consequently of suboptimal quality and use to the student. This outcome is not necessarily a direct consequence of any deficiencies on the part of the advisory network. Instead this scenario may simply represent a "necessary evil," whereby the sheer quantity of students and diversity of their backgrounds and educational experiences precludes their ability to receive high quality support for the full spectrum of challenges that faces prehealth students (for example, coursework, standardized tests, financial aid, extracurricular activities, or personal recommendations).

The current state of undergraduate prehealth advising appears to be simply a means to an end. The advising process is standardized for the purposes of maximizing efficiency and thus nearly identical packets of information and advice are delivered to tens of thousands of students annually. High-quality advising consists of personalized attention with up-to-date recommendations that truly "fit" the student. Identifying this "fit"—a representative picture of the student's interests as defined by the relative emphasis he or she places on academic, extracurricular, and vocational activities—is nearly impossible under the current status quo. Further, advisers' inability to diagnose this fit leads many to prescribe a protocol that is followed too closely by students who believe this advice holds the key to a graduate-school acceptance: volunteer at a local hospital, get research experience, shadow a doctor or nurse or veterinarian, and others on the all-too-familiar list. The current advisory system can place little emphasis on development of the individual. Thus a very unique student who has described his or her undergraduate experience in the "personal statement" on the medical school application begins to sound like the other hundreds of students who used identical advisory services.

That said, could colleges and universities realistically offer focused advice that is aligned with individual goals and unique interests of the student? The answer: probably not under the traditional advising system. There are a number of reasons that the current system is not able to provide information beyond that which can be easily found in any "Preparing for Grad School" book. The primary reason is logistics. It is simply unreasonable for three or four advisers to maintain personal relationships with all prehealth students, a number that can be as high as a few thousand in large universities. With that in mind, the advent of personal mentors into this equation opens doors to the world of complementary advising. General premed advising has demonstrated its ability to provide timely information on the current state of premed requirements, curriculum coordination, and a basic understanding of the application process for graduate school. It has proven less apt at directing students toward opportunities, academic and otherwise, that fit their near and long-term aspirations. The role of mentors in this coordinated effort is to further develop and direct some of the established student interests. The office of undergraduate advising should maintain a pool from a number of disciplines of viable mentors who could each advise a handful of students. Alternatively, students may identify their own mentor from within the university or perhaps from the community. In the end, some combination of this may be most easily achieved. A sample of this model is shown in Table 3.1.

As described above, this complementary system would not be module-based, where students would change advisers when they advanced. Instead, the advising process evolves into a coordinated and dynamic structure capable of managing the multifaceted needs of prehealth students. In particular, this network of advisers could better identify the personality and interests of each student and develop plans (courses, extracurricular activities, and jobs or internships) that could be executed in a coordinated fashion with ease. In addition to students receiving a richer college experience and expanding their résumés, the increased exposure to advising or mentoring resources will be reflected in recommendation letters, calls to deans, and the content of the final application. Each member of this advisory system will play an integral role in ensuring that both near and long-term goals and requirements are met. Once the student's interests have been clearly defined, his or her mentor can effectively assist the student based on expressed interests and past activities.

Table 3.1. Roles in Advising Prehealth Students

General prehealth adviser	Prehealth academic requirements, course scheduling, grad-school information, general reference for short-term undergraduate opportunities. Encourage early exploration of academic interests.
Concentration or major adviser	Information specific to undergraduate major (for example, chemistry, engineering, and so on)
Mentor	Reference for trends in careers, industries. Contact for extracurricular and vocational activities. Ensures activities fit expressed interests and long-term goals.

An alternative scenario might use a university or college's career planning and placement service for its upperclassmen. At this point, most prehealth students have finished a majority of course requirements and are focusing on standardized testing and applications, and some have even begun to seriously look into alternative career paths. Depending on the size and reach of this office, a portion of the burden may be able to shift onto the career planning office.

Clearly the long-term goal is to improve the quality of the prehealth advising process. Ultimately the advising that takes place is really a part of a much larger educational experience. Often, students have been forced to select a course of study or extracurricular activities early in their undergraduate experience to properly prepare for applying to graduate school. In some cases, this process actually begins years before college with advanced-placement examinations and math and science clubs and competitions. Needless to say, given the emphasis that students place on "getting in," it would seem worthwhile for advisers or mentors to make that a primary concern as well. That is, an appropriate advisory system may be able to better assist students in their quest for acceptance in the desired program because it has helped to create an individual, not simply a "premed."

References

Abdelman, W. H., Bryon, D. J., and Davidson, C. S. "A Useful Way to Orient Students to Medical Careers" (letter). *Academy Medicine,* 1995, *70,* 83.

Alexander, S. F., Lyon, L. J., Nevins, M. A., Yere, L. R., Jr., and Thayer, H. S. "Ten Years of Orienting College Students to Careers in Medicine." *Journal of the American Medical Association,* 1992, *267*(24), 3330–3331.

Alexander, S. F., Nevins, M. A., Lyon, L. J., Thayer, H. S., and Yere, L. R., Jr. "A Community Hospital's Program for Premedical Student Orientation." *Journal of the Medical Society of New Jersey,* 1983, *80*(6), 421–422.

Becker, M. H., Katatsky, M. E., and Seidel, H. M. "A Follow-up Study of Unsuccessful Applicants to Medical Schools." *Journal of Medical Education,* 1973, *48,* 991–1001.

Bruhn, J. G. "The Ills of Premedical Advising." *Journal of Medical Education,* 1977, *52,* 676–678.

Bruhn, J. G., Fuentes, R. G., Jr., Trevino, F. M., and Williams, L. B., Jr. "Follow-up of Minority Premedical Students Attending Summer Enrichment Programs in a Medical Setting." *Texas Medicine,* 1976, *72*(8), 87–96.

Caplan, R. M., Kreiter, C., and Albanese, M. "Preclinical Science Course 'Preludes' Taken by Premedical Students: Do They Provide a Competitive Advantage?" *Academy Medicine,* 1996, *71*(8), 920–922.

Elam, C. T., Lenhoff, K., and Johnson, M. M. "Premedical Course Recommendations of Premedical Advisors, Medical Students and Medical School Faculty. *Academy Medicine,* 1997, *72*(1), 72–73.

Gerbens, D. A., Stid, M. A., and Foulds, K. L. "A Collaborative Internship Program for Premedical Students" (letter). *Academy Medicine,* 1998, *73*(8), 827–828.

Hesser, A., Cregler, L. L., and Lewis, L. "Predicting the Admission into Medical School of African American College Students Who Have Participated in Summer Academic Enrichment Programs." *Academy Medicine,* 1998, *73*(2), 187–191.

Imperato, P. J. "The Need for Premedical Curricular Reform" (letter, comment). *Academy Medicine,* 1997, *72*(9), 734–735.

Stimmel, B., Smith, K., and Kase, N. "The Humanities and Medicine Program: The Need for the Traditional Premedical Requirements." *Academy Medicine,* 1995, *70*(5), 438.

Trevino, F. M., Fuentes, R. G., and Bruhn, J. C. "The Premedical Advisory Process: Attitudes of Premedical Advisors. *Texas Medicine,* 1977, *73,* 79–85.

TIMOTHY R. B. JOHNSON *is chair and Bates Professor of Diseases of Women and Children in the Department of Obstetrics and Gynecology, Medical School, research scientist in the Center for Human Growth and Development, and professor in women's studies, College of Literature, Science and the Arts at the University of Michigan, Ann Arbor.*

PHILIP D. SETTIMI *is an honors economics graduate of The University of Michigan, Ann Arbor and a student at the University of Michigan Medical School.*

JULIET L. ROGERS *has an undergraduate degree in political science and a Masters degree in Public Health. She is a doctoral candidate in the Department of Health Management and Policy at the School of Public Health, University of Michigan, Ann Arbor and codirector at the Center of Excellence in Women's Health of the University of Michigan Health System.*

4

Student mentoring in technical disciplines offers some special challenges. This chapter describes how students benefit from mentoring in an engineering curriculum and gives specific examples of student-mentoring programs.

Mentoring in the Technical Disciplines: Fostering a Broader View of Education, Career, and Culture In and Beyond the Workplace

Rose M. Marra, Robert N. Pangborn

Technical disciplines, as represented by programs in higher education dealing with technology and engineering, are facing a unique challenge to respond to the needs of industry and the nation's workforce. New expectations, from the need to increase the diversity in the student mix to the focus on lifelong learning to meet the rapidly changing and expanding technical-knowledge base, have prompted a reexamination of curricular objectives and teaching methodologies. Combined with shifts in the characteristics and motivations of incoming students, there perhaps has never been a more critical need for emphasizing a student-centered approach to education. Central to the refocusing of student learning in a more engaged and active environment is the interaction between the faculty, peer, or professional mentor and the student. The special considerations, objectives, and mechanisms for mentoring in engineering and other technical environments are discussed here, with specific examples of its practice and impact.

Why Mentoring in Engineering?

There are a number of objectives that motivate the interest in mentoring as a key learning tool in the technical disciplines. These include engaging students early in their academic and social development at the college level, helping them clarify their career and life goals, providing appropriate role

NEW DIRECTIONS FOR TEACHING AND LEARNING, no. 85, Spring 2001   © Jossey-Bass, a Wiley company

models—especially for students from groups that are historically underrepresented in the field, and addressing the expectations incorporated in new outcome-based accreditation criteria.

Counteracting Incoming Student Misconceptions. Surveys and reports conducted at institutional and national levels have provided clear evidence that the characteristics of students who enter college are changing. A longitudinal study by the Higher Education Research Institute at UCLA documents the reversal over the past thirty years in high school students' primary motivation for attending college from the desire to develop a meaningful philosophy of life to the pursuit of financial reward (Astin, Parrot, Korn, and Sax, 1997). At Penn State, incoming first-year students cite vocational preparation at twice the rate of intellectual development among the three highest reasons for attending college (The Pennsylvania State University, 1996).

At the same time, there is good evidence that students do not understand what professionals in technical and engineering fields actually do, nor do they have a good picture of the skills and competencies they will need to be successful. Frequently, they underestimate the academic expectations (68 percent of incoming Penn State first-year students anticipate studying twenty hours or less per week); are ambivalent about the importance of the broader, general-education component of their education; and do not recognize the importance of integrating sound communication, interpersonal, and problem-solving skills with the acquisition of technical foundation knowledge. Countering students' unrealistic perceptions of the complement of professional and life skills they will need is critical because, despite projections that technical skills will define the workforce of the future, even the holder of an engineering degree cannot expect to enjoy *job* security. It may be true that those trained in technical fields will have more *employment* security, but only if the employee is willing to abandon notions of comfort and entitlement and accept the new environment of flexibility, group operations, accountability, performance measures, and continuous updating of skills.

Creating Coherent Curricula. The engineering curriculum offers some special challenges to students that underscore and reinforce the importance of mentoring. Engineering's technical nature makes it necessary for students to spend the majority of their first two years in college studying prerequisite fundamentals such as mathematics, physics, and the principles of static and dynamic systems. While developing a strong background in these content-based areas is critical to success in engineering, these courses do not immerse our students in activities that actually "define" engineering. In other words, students do not get a chance to "do engineering" in these courses. Some students naturally lose interest in pursuing engineering during these initial studies. Thus it is vitally important, given the high attrition from engineering in the first two years (Marra and Palmer, 1997), to provide students with a better perspective of the choices and contributions they will be in a position to make. During this time mentoring, from either faculty or other upper-division or graduate students, can help these entering students see future applications of their current studies toward actual engineering careers.

Recruiting a More Diverse Student Population. Underrepresentation of women and minorities in engineering has persisted, despite the advances made in the last decade. In a summary of data compiled by the Engineering Workforce Commission (EWC), Lashley (1997) finds that, while women outnumber men in undergraduate education overall, women accounted for just under 20 percent of all full-time engineering students in fall 1996. Underrepresented minorities (African Americans, Hispanics, and Native Americans) accounted for only 9 percent of first-year, full-time students and 15 percent of all full-time engineering undergraduate students. In the absence of personal attention and appropriate role models, it is unlikely that recruitment and retention of these populations into engineering will continue to be successful. For students to see themselves in the profession, it is necessary for them to have first-hand interactions with those who look like them and can provide a positive and realistic view of the challenges and rewards of pursuing a technical career path. Further, it is well accepted that men and women participate in different ways in the classroom, respond differently to various learning environments, and may be treated differently by the predominantly male faculty (Sandler, Silverberg, and Hall, 1996). Hence, it is important to exploit opportunities for interactions with peers and professional mentors who, by their own experiences and successful examples, can help students develop self-esteem, awareness, and confidence.

Learning Beyond Obligation. Mentoring and other apprentice-type experiences, such as job shadowing and undergraduate research, provide insight into the real world of engineering that students desperately need in those early years. Cooperative education and teaching internships provide students with similar kinds of active exposure to real practice—industrial and academic, respectively—while they're still in school where the stakes aren't as high and mistakes are an expected part of the learning process.

Offering Rewards Beyond Grades. One of the distinctions of mentoring, in comparison with many other forums for learning, is that it occurs or should occur in a nonjudgmental environment, free of the prospect of either reward or threat of grades and other academic consequences. Released from the confines of the classroom and curricular content, these relationships reveal the culture of the profession and life beyond the work environment, allow risk-free interchange of aspirations and avocations, disclose the faculty to be truly interested in their students, and foster the nurturing of creative talents and instincts.

Defining, Measuring, and Achieving Educational Outcomes. Aside from the advantage that the personal interaction implicit in mentoring provides for students, it can be seen as a key element in addressing the new educational expectations being implemented in engineering. The new "Engineering

Criteria 2000" formulated by the national Accreditation Board for Engineering and Technology (1997) focuses on constituent input, the formation of measurable program outcomes, outcome assessment, and the process by which continuous curricular improvement is effected. The change in emphasis from documenting what we are teaching students to providing clear evidence of what students *can do* as a result of their education will require that faculty members know the students better. The enterprise of teaching will need to be supplemented with mechanisms that allow us to establish the depth of the learning that has occurred. The one-on-one interactions typical of mentoring will serve as a conduit for both learning and evaluation of the demonstrable outcome of the teaching and learning process.

What Constitutes Mentoring?

Mentoring can occur in many forms: student to student (upper division to lower division, or graduate to undergraduate), faculty member to student, and industry professional to student. In all cases, these kinds of relationships have advantages that can be particularly meaningful in engineering. They provide informal and formal opportunities for students to think, exchange ideas, and receive guidance about the curriculum and profession. They constitute a framework for cognitive apprenticeship (meaning that what one is apprenticing for is a skill or process in the cognitive domain rather than in traditional apprenticeship domains such as artistry, cooking, or other skilled occupations) and increase the student's sense of responsibility for learning that transcends the conventional motivation and rewards for academic performance. And finally, they can broaden the educational experience by providing personal examples that help cultivate students' understanding of their future as not only embracing professional milestones but including citizenship, service, and personal growth as well.

Mentoring occurs in both formal and informal settings. Traditional forms of academic advising, if pushed beyond the boundaries of curricular counseling, and classroom teaching, if seeded with rich historical examples or personal experiences, can both take on significant aspects of mentoring. Integrating one's research into classroom instruction, encouraging student participation, and providing feedback on students' work can expand students' horizons and initiate dialogues that promote excitement in learning and understanding of professional traditions, conventions, and culture. Transforming the classroom environment through active learning and team-based activities further reduces the students' or instructor's anonymity. Mentoring can also occur when faculty members get involved with students outside the classroom. Faculty participation with student organizations and projects, activities in residence halls, invitations to work in the laboratory or attend a professional conference, and development of programs that feature interaction with industry professionals provide exposure to scholarly dimensions that are not easily built into the traditional forum.

Educational research has shown some of the broader benefits of various mentoring activities. For instance, advising and orientation programs can affect graduation rates. Forrest (1985) found that institutions with the most comprehensive set of orientation and advising programs had a graduation rate 9 percent higher than a comparative set of institutions with the least comprehensive array of these programs. Undergraduate research—which affords another forum for mentoring—is a positive predictor of graduate school attendance and enhances preparation for graduate or professional studies (Astin, 1993).

How Do We Make It Happen?

While successful mentoring may require support from administrators, the key ingredient to fostering student-mentor relationships is developing the comfort level and ability of the peer, faculty member, or practitioner who acts as the mentor. Students clearly thirst for such interactions and place a high value on the expression of faculty interest in them (Willits, Moore, and Enerson, 1997). But potential or prospective mentors are not always confident with or knowledgeable in the mechanics of functioning as a mentor, especially in relation to undergraduates.

Regardless of the discipline, good mentoring requires interpersonal skills such as attentive listening, assertiveness, feedback methods, and positive reinforcement techniques (Wunsch, 1994). Whether mentoring occurs via a formal program or simply through student contact during advising, orientation programs, first-year seminars, or instructors' office hours, these skills will strengthen a mentor's effectiveness. These are not skills that potential mentors necessarily possess. Several training approaches can be used to prepare faculty and others for mentoring relationships.

• Since mentoring *can* take place during well-run office hours and advising sessions, explicit faculty training in these activities can be fruitful. Workshops with new faculty should include discussions with experienced and highly skilled advisers and teachers. In addition to developing advising skills, such training allows new faculty to learn to appreciate the importance these interactions have to students.

• First-year seminars afford entering students opportunities to get to know a faculty member just as they begin their studies. Such interactions can be quite influential for new students, increasing their awareness of what is expected of them and that the faculty does really want them to be successful. Faculty development focused on teaching first-year seminars is crucial, as many instructors may be teaching first-year students for the first time in their careers. Workshops and other development programs allow seasoned faculty to discuss and demonstrate effective methods of working with first-year students to develop the self-esteem and confidence needed to succeed in engineering.

• Finally, protégés can also be trained in productive mentor behavior. Whether the mentor relationship is a formal or informal one, protégés should be aware of their own goals and should also have realistic expectations about what the mentor relationship can offer (Wilson, 1994; Wunsch, 1994).

Mentoring Examples

The College of Engineering at Penn State has developed a number of models for mentoring that address the specific needs of our students and characteristics of the discipline. Several illustrations are provided below.

• The increase in courses involving active learning, including team-based introductions to design and a first-year seminar program for incoming students, case- and problem-based courses in the second and third years, and group-oriented capstone design projects in the senior year, all provide opportunities for mentoring. Since many of these activities involve report writing, development of presentations, participation in design competitions, and travel to regional or national conferences, the potential interactions between faculty and undergraduates increasingly mirror those that faculty have always had with graduate students. For instance, meeting with students to review, guide, or provide feedback on draft reports offers fertile ground for discussing the processes inherent to scholarly inquiry and the creative enterprise of scientific discovery and application. It also furnishes an opportunity to create an explicit link between students' engineering courses and the general education component of their studies. Such conversations can help students realize the ethical, environmental, and cultural considerations of all engineering decisions. Further, even the act of faculty and students traveling together to conferences or competitions sets the stage for interchange on subjects that are less-easily approached or accommodated in the formal classroom setting (for example, contemporary issues, traditions in the discipline, and workplace and societal conventions).

• The Women in Engineering Program (WEP) offers a variety of mentoring and networking programs. All are designed to introduce undergraduate and graduate women students to each other and to women faculty and alumnae in their disciplines. The programs provide a forum for the participants to discuss academic, social, and career-related issues. The alumnae e-mail mentoring program, or "e-mentoring," is specifically designed to pair up women engineering students with women engineering alumni. The alumni who participate are coached on what types of interactions are most beneficial to students and initiate the mentoring relationship with an introductory e-mail to their protégé. Students are then able to respond with a statement of their educational and career goals—and thus the dialog begins. Ultimately, the program provides women engineering students who may not have the opportunity to work with many, if any, female professional engineers during their schooling with role models in their own field. Such interactions have proved to be effective in developing and maintaining students' confidence and interest in becoming engineers.

• The undergraduate teaching intern program is an example of a mentoring activity that includes both student-to-student and faculty-to-student aspects (Marra and Litzinger, 1997). Each undergraduate teaching intern (TI) works with an engineering faculty member to assist in teaching an undergraduate course. TIs are not simply undergraduate versions of graduate teaching assistants. Rather, the intern's duties are structured to provide an opportunity to try out a faculty member's teaching-related responsibilities, such as holding office hours, running out-of-class supplemental instruction sessions, doing *limited* amounts of grading, writing test and quiz items, and teaching two or more classes during the semester. Mentoring occurs both *for* the TIs and *by* the TIs. Faculty members provide mentoring for the TIs in the form of regular meetings to help them prepare for assisting students on homework and for test preparation. Via such interactions, the TIs get to know a faculty member much better than in normal faculty-student interactions, and specifically to understand what it is like to *be* an engineering faculty member. Finally the TIs, who are upper-division engineering students, provide mentoring for the undergraduates in their assigned course. These students benefit both from the TI providing an example of a successful upper-division student acting as an expert in a particular engineering discipline and from the TI's ability to provide explanations that are often clearer to their fellow undergraduate students.

Conclusions

Student mentoring in engineering provides a service that many students crave. Recent interviews with senior engineering students elicited these comments on how students envision the role of the faculty member. This student notes the benefits of conducting undergraduate research: "But just doing research work with a professor . . . doing undergraduate research— that was definitely really helpful." Another student spoke of the importance of being able to interact with faculty more spontaneously in a class or laboratory setting: ". . . little bit before the lab's due so concurrently you see that professor several times not just going in [during] office hours [or] whatever and things come up when you're in class and you start thinking about it. . . . You get a chance to ask him about it." And finally this student uses the metaphor of a physician with medical school students to describe a desirable way for faculty to interact with and mentor students: ". . . when they're off duty they all went to a pub and the doctor would basically hold court. If you wanted to talk about why he chose to treat with this instead of that, or why he chose this method, that was open. If you wanted to ask him what he's doing this weekend, that was open. It was more of bringing the students up to the level of the instructor. And everything was done in a very open manner."

Clearly, there are many faculty members who would and do engage in activities similar to those described by these students but, at the same time, faculty at a research-focused institution such as Penn State struggle with the rewards for engaging in such activities. Certainly, good mentoring can be enabled via the opportunities for student contact previously described and accompanied by mentor training. Productive mentoring programs will more likely grow when mentors—particularly faculty mentors—have a clear sense of both the intrinsic and extrinsic rewards for such practices.

Apprentice-type relationships have particular value in engineering where we strive to help students develop as capable and creative problem solvers cognizant of broader social implications while they are still in an environment where the consequences of mistakes and failures are an increased opportunity for learning.

References

Accreditation Board for Engineering and Technology (ABET). "Engineering Criteria 2000: Criteria for Accrediting Programs in Engineering in the United States." *ASEE Prism,* 1997, 6(7), 41–42.

Astin, A. W. *What Matters in College? Four Critical Years Revisited.* San Francisco: Jossey-Bass, 1993.

Astin, A. W., Parrot, S. A., Korn, W. S., and Sax, L. J. *The American Freshman: Thirty-Year Trends.* Los Angeles: Higher Education Research Institute, 1997.

Forrest, A. "Creating Conditions for Student and Institutional Success." In L. Noel, D. Levitz and D. Saluri (eds.). *Increasing Student Retention: Effective Programs and Practices for Reducing the Dropout Rate.* San Francisco: Jossey-Bass, 1985.

Lashley, P. "Enrollments 96: Inching Downwards." *ASEE Prism,* 1997, 7(1), 35–37.

Marra, R. M. and Litzinger, T. A. "A Model for Implementing Supplemental Instruction in Engineering." Paper presented at the Frontiers in Education Conference (FIE), Pittsburgh, Pa., 1997.

Marra, R. M. and Palmer, E. "College of Engineering 1996–97 Retention Study." University Park, Pa.: The Pennsylvania State University, 1997.

Pennsylvania State University, The. "Freshman Academic Profile 1995–1996." University Park, Pa.: The Pennsylvania State University, 1996.

Sandler, B. R., Silverberg, L. A., and Hall, R. M. *The Chilly Classroom Climate: A Guide to Improve the Education of Women.* Washington, D.C.: National Association for Women in Education, 1996.

Willits, F. K., Moore, B. L., and Enerson, D. "Quality of Instruction: Surveys of Students and Teachers at University Park." University Park, Pa.: The Pennsylvania State University, 1997.

Wilson, K. B. "Developing a Freshman Mentoring Program: A Small College Experience." In M. A. Wunsch (ed.). *Mentoring Revisited: Making an Impact on Individuals and Institutions.* New Directions in Teaching and Learning, no. 57. San Francisco: Jossey-Bass, 1994.

Wunsch, M. A., "Developing Mentor Programs: Major Themes and Issues." In M. A. Wunsch (ed.). *Mentoring Revisited: Making an Impact on Individuals and Institutions.* New Directions in Teaching and Learning, no. 57. San Francisco: Jossey-Bass, 1994.

ROSE M. MARRA *is assistant professor in the School of Information Science and Learning Technologies, University of Missouri-Columbia.*

ROBERT N. PANGBORN *is associate dean for undergraduate studies and professor of engineering mechanics in the College of Engineering, The Pennsylvania State University.*

5

This chapter focuses on the importance of international study in American universities and on how to mentor students to develop a global perspective.

International Study for Outstanding Students: A Case Study

Mary Gage

As the twenty-first century begins we find ourselves living in a world nearly devoid of boundaries. We turn on the television, open newspapers, cruise the Web, and gather information from every corner of every continent. In business, diplomacy, journalism, and strategic affairs, it is now more important than ever to produce future leaders who understand the intricacies of other cultures and other languages, and universities have a unique responsibility to give their students a sound international education.

The Undergraduate Fellowships Office

My task at The Pennsylvania State University is to work with academically outstanding students. Our previous president realized that some of Penn State's best students might be at a disadvantage because, unlike students at small liberal arts colleges, they might go through their whole four years in large classes without any personal mentoring. As a partial remedy, he created the Undergraduate Fellowships Office (UFO) to encourage suitable students to apply for national scholarships, and in 1992 I was given the task of creating that office. I have worked with wonderful young people who are as impressive as their counterparts at the most prestigious private universities, because often they achieved academic excellence in spite of rather than because of the prevailing undergraduate culture. Often no mentor had guided them into the laboratory or the library; they have used their elbows and knees to get research positions. By the time I meet them, they have already proved themselves self-motivated scholars, committed to their chosen areas of study.

I try to identify outstanding students early in their undergraduate careers so that I can alert them to suitable scholarship opportunities. The admissions office helps by sending a list of the forty incoming freshmen with the highest SAT scores. This allows the honors college to forge connections to its most academically successful freshmen, and faculty members may identify some of their most promising students.

The Case for International Study

While it would be desirable for all students to take part in international study programs, they will often opt not to participate. Many students are the first in their families to attend college. They may come from a one-hundred-acre farm in western Pennsylvania or from inner city Philadelphia; they may never have traveled outside the state, let alone the nation. Their parents may not hold passports and the only news they hear about the world is negative. What would be the point of learning a language they cannot imagine using, and maybe delaying graduation and entry into the workforce by a whole year just to pursue international study? Why leave friends and family behind and go somewhere unfamiliar and alien to their sensibilities?

The mentoring process begins with a discussion of how students might make the best use of their time at Penn State. There is a tendency for really bright students to drop their cocurricular activities once they move from high school to college, in order to focus on their studies. However, it's likely that they will have a much more rewarding experience if they continue to develop their interests both in and out of the classroom. International study should be regarded as an essential part of a multifaceted undergraduate experience that includes, but does not take precedence over, cocurricular activities such as community service, music, writing, and participation in sports.

Efforts to get these future leaders to study in another country tie in with Penn State's plan to internationalize the university. One goal is for 20 percent of any graduating class to have participated in international study and the proportion has now risen to around 11 percent. In addition to contributing to this overarching goal, there is a more prosaic reason for promoting international study. If these students decide to compete for national scholarships, they will be much more likely to win them if they have a full résumé as well as first-hand experience of another language and culture.

There is a choice of 105 international programs giving direct credit toward a degree at Penn State. To study, work, and live in another culture as a young, unattached adult is a mind-opening endeavor, and students will learn at least as much outside their classes as in them. Because their peers are the most effective advocates for international study, e-mail messages are shared from other Penn State students describing their time in various international destinations as the most valuable experience of their entire undergraduate career. Examples of recently returned students sharing stories include an electrical engineering student from Egypt with a transformed view of Arab culture and an architecture student from Prague so inspired by the buildings that he is applying for scholarships to return. These students have a fresh perspective that has transformed their view of themselves and their place in the world and the United States.

How to Choose an International Study Program

Once persuaded to consider international study, students should be directed toward a program that matches their needs. Those who have never traveled to another country or are not yet fluent in a second language may be better off on an "island" program, where students travel in a group and are taught separately by teachers familiar with the U.S. system of education. They can use this opportunity to expose themselves to the prevailing culture by joining local societies, sharing dormitories with native speakers, or lodging with host families. Whenever possible, students should consider the option of exchange programs in which they drop into an international university, indistinguishable from other students. Only by immersing themselves in this way can they truly learn another language and take part in another culture's social and academic life, frequently making friends and contacts that will last a lifetime.

Exchange programs may be the ideal way for students to study internationally, but there are many complex curricula that allow little opportunity to spend a semester or year in another country. For students in such rigorous majors, an appropriate choice might be short-term immersion in another culture. Popular and successful short programs, such as a tropical biology course in Costa Rica, occur during the winter break or the summer vacation. These programs not only give international opportunities to students who could not otherwise fit them into their curricula, they also allow adventurous students to experience something different. For example, engineering students may go on the London theatre program or the Mexican and Italian art history programs and find refreshing ways to step outside their majors.

Because many professionally oriented students are particularly focused, an international internship is an excellent way to get a taste of the global workplace. International business students can learn about British business practices at the University of Manchester, England, before experiencing them first-hand through internships with British firms. National consortia run inventive programs, such as the Institute of International Education's Global Engineering Education Exchange, where engineers study before completing international internships.

Altruistic students who enjoy helping others through volunteer activity can join programs run by service-learning agencies such as Volunteers for Peace. In these programs, students can spend a summer helping others and gaining international experience at the same time. Students live in work camps along with volunteers from many other countries, helping communities in ways as varied as building basketball courts in Mexico, organizing consciousness-raising groups on concentration camp sites in Germany, or developing plays to promote peace in the Netherlands. These varied and individualized experiences can be intense and even life-altering for the right students, instigating some to seek out additional experience in agencies like the Peace Corps, and leading them to careers in areas like international development or with agencies such as the State Department.

Finding the Money for International Study

By being offered such a varied menu, students can be attracted to international programs, but there remains the major problem of paying for these costly opportunities. While Penn State keeps tuition for international study at the same rate as its own in-state tuition, students must consider fares and sometimes higher living costs. They often have to leave behind a job. I encourage students to start by exploring financial aid within the university. At Penn State, there is some help for traditionally disadvantaged students to study overseas and, thanks to a generous benefactor, one large endowment finances international travel grants for up to 150 honors students a year.

Some of the external scholarships pay directly for international study. The National Security Education Program (NSEP) is for undergraduates who aspire to be future leaders in business, science, engineering, and international politics. It awards money for all kinds of international study in countries outside Western Europe, Canada, and Australasia. These stipends range from a summer program for freshmen and sophomores to semester- or year-long programs for upperclassmen. Students can also benefit from finding suitable offerings at other schools and consortia as well as from Penn State. For example, one freshman started her study of Mandarin in Beijing and a junior enrolled in Brazilian business internships. The NSEP has a service component, which requires winners to complete a paid internship with a government agency for the same length of time that they spend on their international study program. This can be a useful experience for students interested in strategic and public policy, and can lead to employment within their area of interest.

Penn State students have had the most success with the U.S. Student Fulbright Program, which sends graduating seniors and graduate students to study, do research, or teach in another country for one academic year. This program is a wonderful vehicle for outstanding students who use their own initiative to set up an international project. More than one hundred Penn State students have gained grants through this program since the Undergraduate Fellowships Office began in 1992. They have studied lizards in Crete, tuba playing in Sweden, stars in Australia, pharmaceuticals in Singapore, and transportation in West Africa. No matter the field of study, the experience often leads to long-term relationships between Fulbright grantees and their international mentors.

The Advantages of International Study

International study is certainly an asset for any national scholarship applicant. If students have traveled to other countries to further their interests, they already demonstrate concrete evidence of their energy and initiative that makes all the difference on their applications. Even in purely academic scholarships, international study helps to ensure an applicant's success. The Jacob S. Javits Fellowship, for example, awards money to cover four years' graduate study in the arts, humanities, and social sciences. One of Penn State's recent winners was an excellent young philosopher, but a unique element of her application was that during the summer of her junior year, she had paid her own way to study Greek language and philosophy at the University of Toronto.

International Awareness across the University

Through the Undergraduate Fellowships Office, outstanding Penn State students now win about sixty national scholarships a year, of which approximately one-half are for international study. International study, however, is the tip of the iceberg when it comes to internationalizing a university: a far more daunting challenge is to internationalize the campus.

At Penn State, we have to work very hard on this issue since the university is unusually homogeneous, particularly at the undergraduate level. In the past six years, for example, we have managed to double the number of international undergraduates at Penn State to approximately five hundred. We have to move forward on many fronts to try to enrich our students' international awareness and experience, both in and out of the classroom. The curriculum, the heart of any academic institution, has to be a focus of our efforts. Minors in international studies, second-language acquisition, and cross-disciplinary courses are all appearing alongside international study. We are developing international exchange programs not only as the best way to immerse U.S. students in other cultures, but also as a valuable way to import international students into Penn State. We try to use our international faculty members as well as our three thousand international graduate students to lecture and stage international festivals on campus. One organization on campus encourages volunteers to host international visitors, pairs Penn State students with international students as language partners, and sends international students to speak to local schoolchildren.

In these ways we work to enhance international awareness. Our work only forms one tiny part of a massive structure, but it is intensely rewarding to mentor a student from a rural or inner city background who could never otherwise afford to study in a foreign, exciting atmosphere. We know other universities across the nation are also producing outstanding international citizens, and this knowledge reassures that future graduates will increasingly possess the necessary global perspective.

MARY GAGE is an affiliate associate professor in the College of Communications who runs the Undergraduate Fellowships Office at The Pennsylvania State University, University Park.

6

This chapter considers mentoring in mass communication and journalism programs in which the dual objectives of professional and liberal arts education are often addressed by faculty recruited from the professions as well as from backgrounds of graduate education and research scholarship.

Mentoring Undergraduates with Professional and Liberal Arts Goals: The Mass Communication Experience

Jeremy Cohen

Mass communication and journalism programs offer especially fertile ground for mentoring relationships among students, faculty, staff, and others. Undergraduates, and graduate students too, have much to gain from educators who can develop journeyman-apprentice associations. Mentors guide students toward professional careers in fields such as journalism, advertising, Web-based media, and the information sciences and technologies, where there will be immediate expectations of their performance and technical abilities and of their understanding of the unique responsibilities, institutional cultures, and practices within those fields. The special place of the liberal arts in communication also makes mentoring a teaching and learning method, well-suited to the goals of communication educators. Also, an increased understanding of a scholarship of teaching that recognizes and stresses the value of active and engaged learning supports the usefulness of mentoring relationships to deeper learning and personal development among students.

Mentoring to Engage the Liberal Arts

Philosopher Alexander Meiklejohn articulated the liberal arts goal in a series of three lectures delivered at the University of Chicago and published in 1948 as *Political Freedom: The Constitutional Powers of the People*. "A primary task of American education," he wrote, "is to arouse and to cultivate, in all the members of the body politic, a desire to understand what our national plan of government is" (p. 3). Meiklejohn viewed the liberal arts as the basis of understanding the American democratic plan. He viewed civic participation as a political duty inherent in that plan. And he saw unfettered communication through the media as a means of carrying out the duties he associated with each citizen's democratic political compact.

Meiklejohn's understanding of the relationships among open communication, an educated public, and our democratic system of governance is reflected today in the publicly stated missions of most colleges and departments of mass communication and journalism. It resides in their core and in the commonly accepted accreditation standards that require a mix in which three fourths of a student's courses will be in liberal arts, the remaining quarter in the major.

Also reflected today in the surveys and research that describe a majority of college students, however, are attitudes anathema to mass communication educational goals integrating the curriculum with liberal arts and democratic participation. The predominant interest among students, Arthur Levine and Jeannette Cureton report, is not the arts of liberty, but consumerism (Levine and Cureton, 1998). The practice of political participation among students is vanishing (Sax, Astin, Korn, and Mahoney, 1997).

The problem may be especially acute in communication. Professional programs attract students with strong vocational goals who want to master the skills they will need and move quickly to the professional practices of writing, editing, and visual media. For these students, time spent immersed in the liberal arts can seem like time wasted. Furthermore, the ethics of the communication classroom and the newsroom often discourage overt political participation in favor of the neutrality needed to foster journalistic objectivity. Personal participation in civic affairs by journalists is often viewed as a threat to journalistic independence. When the explicit message is "neutrality," the more subtle messages of civic participation that reach beyond the private cloister of the voting booth are easily overlooked.

How are we to overcome attitudes of consumerism and political apathy while simultaneously achieving an increasingly comprehensive academic mission? According to its catalogue my own institution, the largest communication college in the nation, "recognizes its mission to educate students for citizenship in a society in which communication and information are a major commodity and the basis of the democratic process" (Pennsylvania State University, 2000, p. 254). It also accepts the charge to prepare students for employment, and embraces the goal of teaching sophisticated practices in the gathering, analysis, and dissemination of information.

Any expectation of accomplishing all of this in four years (or five as is now so often the case) should raise doubts about everything else in the catalogue. Some things require time, aging, and experience, as well as exposure, and that is the fundamental concept behind mentoring.

Reflection

An apprentice needs more than simple exposure to an exhibition of skills and ideas. The most inspired lecture on the landmark 1964 case *New York Times* v. *Sullivan* is not in and of itself enough to instill a rich grasp of Rev. Martin Luther King, Jr.'s civil rights leadership or of the Supreme Court's First Amendment ruling that breathed life into Dr. King's pacifist tenets. Deep learning also requires reflection and analysis with a master who possesses the experience to guide the student past superficial understandings.

A mentor can encourage an apprentice to reflect on the implications of readings and experiences in ways that will have lasting consequence far beyond a semester's course notes. A mentor can help a student to understand journalism, for example, not as a set of vocational skills but as a means of civic participation. It is an act of simple observation that the *New York Times* aided the cause of democracy by covering Dr. King and the civil rights movement in the South in the 1950s and 1960s. It is enlightenment, however, to reflect on and come to understand Dr. King's logic of nonviolence to achieve political freedom. Dr. King believed readers would be touched by the plight of people of color when they learned through the press what it was to be discriminated against under color of law. They would learn through the press. They would act on that knowledge as an element of civic duty. And in their actions all people would come to share the freedoms otherwise denied them.

Dr. King's rhetoric is eloquent, but not simple. Its roots are to be found in the complex tapestry of the liberal arts such as Meiklejohn's concept of education, Mohandas Gandhi's nonviolent approach to ending British rule in India, the political tracts of the American Revolution, and Samuel Jennings' 1792 painting entitled *Liberty Displaying the Arts and Sciences,* in which, as historian Eric Foner describes it, "The female figure of Liberty offers books to newly freed slaves" (1998, p. 30).

The weave of the professional communication education is similarly eloquent and, like Dr. King's philosophy, far from simple. Students need guidance in order to make the connections necessary to understand the complex relationship between the liberal arts and the professions they seek to enter. Effective learning of this sort requires mentoring, a connection in which educators help students to learn and to perform the practice of reflecting on their discoveries, whether gained through readings or through first-hand experiences.

"The one-on-one interaction that develops between experienced practitioner and aspirant is more like training than teaching; it resembles the journeyman-apprentice relationship that once characterized the artisan guilds," wrote former Stanford University president Donald Kennedy (1997, p. 97). Mentoring does more than show the apprentice how the scholar performs her work. Kennedy and others take to heart the aphorism that the best learning occurs not simply by doing but by thinking about what it is we have done. In communication education the complexity of our mission demands approaches with goals such as the transformation of students from observers to colleagues who are capable of mentoring.

Supporting Clinical-Research Distinctions with Professional Mentoring

The duality of our charge—liberal arts and professional practices—and the mix of academic and professional backgrounds of our faculties have created tensions in mass communication and journalism education. The forces created by this mix are sometimes healthy, sometimes tightly packed with misunderstandings and mistrust between those who view themselves as members of the academic community and those who claim an allegiance to the professional world. The controversial report *Winds of Change* (Medsger, 1996), for example, calls for a pendulum swing that will reduce the number of Ph.D.s and increase the number of communication-industry professionals who fill the ranks of the faculty. The logic is that industry-experienced practitioners are better able to teach and mentor students preparing to enter their fields than are those whose preparation for teaching is purely academic.

Professors and Industry Professionals. Any consideration of mentoring in mass communication and journalism education requires consideration of who is doing the mentoring and whether the professional-professorial distinction is a valid consideration. On the surface at least there appears be a clash between differing cultures with divergent values. "There is too much gloom imparted by [Ph.D.] journalism educators about the future of newspapers and television news," the introduction to *Winds of Change* admonishes (Medsger, 1996). The report was prepared by a respected former journalist, Betty Medsger, who is now a well-regarded journalism professor.

Taken to extremes, there is a dichotomy that can and does lead to intractable faculty feuds and subsequent student confusion. Mentoring from one perspective means preparing to defend the press, to write under deadline, and to embrace newsroom values that have over time come to grips with issues such as advertiser influence on editorial judgment, the rush to scoop the competition, and the influence of technology on journalism. From another perspective, the task of the mentor is to prepare novitiates to challenge communication industry norms, to ask "what might be" instead of "what is," and to embrace discovery in ways not easily suited to the daily routines of the information professions.

Is the student to be left to choose between professor and professional? One response is to answer with a different question, one that strives to cut down the straw-man nature of the professorial-professional dichotomy. What is the mentor's charge? The question is not a new one. Other professions, from law to nursing and engineering to meteorology, already have experience with the preparation of students for the professional realm and already have embraced the integration of clinicians drawn from practice and researchers enlisted from the academy.

Mentoring for the Professions. Lee Shulman, president of the Carnegie Foundation for the Advancement of Teaching, has spent much of his career conducting research focused on how we educate men and women for the professions of teaching and medicine. Rather than taking sides with practicing teachers and physicians or with college professors who teach those practices, Shulman suggests that an alternative question is more useful. He asks in "Professing the Liberal Arts" (Shulman, 1997), what is our charge when we are responsible for the professional learning of students? The mentor's task, in Shulman's framing of the issue, is limited neither to socializing students to the norms of the profession nor to the seemingly esoteric minutia of academic research. Rather, Shulman says, the charge is to act as professional educators, and to profess within our own areas of inquiry and discovery.

Shulman's review of the literature identifies six characteristics that compose the substance of professional school education. The professions exist, he says, to serve social needs and so students must be instructed in what those needs are in order to reach a moral understanding of the professions themselves. Professions are based on bodies of knowledge that are tested and transformed in universities. Much of the special knowledge used in professions has roots in the university, but claims of knowledge begun at the academy must pass the ultimate test of value in practice. Professionals must practice judgment as well as possess knowledge. Professionals begin their work with university-acquired knowledge, but they also must learn to learn from experience—the hallmark of a journeyman. And finally, Shulman says, professionals are recognized and granted special standing because they belong to specialized communities, entrance to which requires a core of skills and knowledge.

The Mentor as Professional. Like medicine, journalism, law, and other professions, teaching is a practice served best by those who have a core of skills, knowledge, judgment, values, and experiences that enable them to apply their expertise successfully to the task of teaching. Whether he or she emerged from the graduate academy or the newsroom, the communication professor's charge is to mentor students in preparation for careers as professionals and to do so in a context cognizant of the liberal arts.

The question of who is best prepared to mentor must not focus on academic versus communication professional in a manner that distracts from the core issue—is the individual adequately and professionally prepared to teach and to mentor? As a first principle, the mentor's task is to be a professional educator. Some will need special expertise and skill in clinical and performance areas such as multimedia design or computer-assisted reporting. Others will need depth in First Amendment theory or media effects. Whatever the area of personal inquiry and discovery, however, every communication educator owes an allegiance to the professionalism of *teaching*.

Communication mentors must possess, in addition to their expertise in the substantive knowledge and practice domains of communication, a core of skills and knowledge about teaching and learning sufficient to earn recognition and standing as members of the teaching profession.

Opportunities to Mentor

The image of a mentor calls to mind Kennedy's reference to artisan and aspirant engaged in a one-on-one interaction. A far different image is invoked by Harvard professor Parker Palmer in his recent book, *The Courage to Teach* (1998). Among his most memorable mentors, Palmer says, was an individual "who lectured at such length and with such enthusiasm, that he left little room for questions and comments" (p. 22).

There is no single definition for or universally accepted defining characteristic of a mentor. Palmer is correct. A mentor might well be a lecturer in a large class who does not know each of the students by their names. There are, however, some characteristics of mentoring that can be identified as essential to a successful mentoring relationship.

Mentoring is a means of developing active and engaged learning among students. The mentor's task is not to serve as a role model, but to engage students in a process of careful reflection. An inspiring lecture may teach students well and serve for some as a role model of everything from careful researcher to thoughtful scholar.

Mentoring, rather than telling or role modeling alone, includes an active relationship between student and teacher in which the mentor provides the opportunity for guided reflection. That need not include face-to-face conversation. A role model lecturer will share valuable insights. A mentor will create assignments around those lectures and insights that involve the student directly. The goal will not be simple awareness of the professor's insight, but self-understanding by the student. Good writing teachers have long served as mentors. Their comments on student papers do not stop with "good idea" or "awkward construction" or the infamous "sp." for spelling error. Truly constructive comments direct the student toward a consideration and understanding of the consequences of their intellectual choices, their choice of words, and their selection of topics. They involve the student in the process itself.

A mentoring relationship need not be face to face. An educator can create the relationship through the use of carefully constructed assignments that include feedback aimed not only at evaluation, but at formative development as well. Key in any case, however, is the existence of a relationship. The mentor and student enter a compact in which the teacher agrees to do more than show and tell and the student agrees to do more than memorize and repeat. Each must agree that the goal is for the student to learn to learn from the experiences undertaken as well as to learn basic skills and information.

Conclusions

At a reception and orientation for new students, I was invited to give a short talk on what the students should expect from their professors and what their professors would expect from them. I invited a former student, Damian, to come with me and asked him to share his own recollections. "When I began, I asked Professor Cohen everything," Damian said. "I wanted his approval and his advice. He was my mentor until one day he answered me by saying, 'You don't need to ask me. You've grown beyond that.' He was right and that was the best part of his mentoring, letting me grow beyond it."

A professional mentor brings to her or his calling a core of skills and knowledge about teaching and learning sufficient to earn recognition and standing as a member of the teaching profession. In communication a mentor always has one eye on the curricular mission of meaningfully integrating the liberal arts with the substantive domains of the profession and a sense of responsibility for introducing students to the skills and knowledge and moral service expectations of the profession. In the end mentoring may be as simple as finding the means to enable students to discover new knowledge and skills and to reflect upon them. And finally, the good mentor is the teacher who knows when the job is complete, knows when the student has learned to learn, and knows then to welcome the student no longer as a pupil, but as a colleague.

References

Foner, E. *The Story of American Freedom.* New York: Norton, 1998.

Kennedy, D. *Academic Duty.* Cambridge, Mass.: Harvard University Press, 1997.

Levine, A., and Cureton, J. *When Hope and Fear Collide: A Portrait of Today's College Student.* San Francisco: Jossey-Bass, 1998.

Medsger, B. *Winds of Change: Challenges Confronting Journalism Education.* Arlington, Va.: Freedom Forum, 1996.

Meiklejohn, A. *Political Freedom: The Constitutional Powers of the People.* Westport, Conn.: Harper and Brothers, 1948.

Palmer, P. *The Courage to Teach.* San Francisco: Jossey-Bass, 1998.

Pennsylvania State University. *Penn State 2000-02 Undergraduate Degree Programs Bulletin.* University Park, Pa.: The Pennsylvania State University, 2000.

Sax, L. J., Astin, A., Korn, W., and Mahoney, K. *The American Freshman: National Forms for Fall 1997.* Los Angeles: UCLA Higher Education Research Institute, 1997.

Shulman, L. "Professing the Liberal Arts." In R. Orril (ed.). *Education and Democracy: Reimagining Liberal Learning in America.* New York: College Entrance Examination Board, 1997.

JEREMY COHEN is associate vice provost for undergraduate education and professor of communications at The Pennsylvania State University. He is coeditor of the Journal of General Education.

7

A science faculty member at a major research university discusses strategic approaches to mentoring undergraduate students within a holistic framework of personal and professional development. This chapter describes the concept of a coordinated mentoring effort across years and disciplines.

Full Human Presence: A Guidepost to Mentoring Undergraduate Science Students

Brian P. Coppola

Hovering over the detailed recommendations for successful mentoring relationships are a few big ideas. Above other things, faculty mentors are obliged to help students uncover their dreams and realize their potentials. Students come to us with their futures wide open with possibilities. Since mentoring cannot be separated from its academic context, work with students in higher education must address explicitly the variety of cultures that intersect at our institutions. Compared with universities of the past, the new multicultural *multiversity* contributes significantly to these cultural intersections. The simple problem of scale is another contributing factor. Many institutions are sprawling places where disciplinary differentiation, hence dis-integration, dominates the physical and intellectual structures. Reintegration to address dis-integration is a worthy goal (Coppola and Daniels, 1998). The seeds of reintegration are found in the growing tendency toward multi- and interdisciplinary work that can reunify the multiversity and have a direct impact on institutional as well as individual faculty and student identities. The role we assume as mentors is one of these identities.

The life of an academic scientist today means taking on roles that were either less demanding or nonexistent in times past. Time to sit and reflect, to carefully guide the education of students at a natural pace—these classic academic responsibilities can conflict with newer demands: seeking competitive funding, pursuing research agendas driven by predicting the "hot" area of investigation, and accumulating students, papers, and citations as a measure of scholarship. Carl Djerassi has characterized the "tribal culture

NEW DIRECTIONS FOR TEACHING AND LEARNING, no. 85, Spring 2001 © Jossey-Bass, a Wiley company

of research scientists" as an "overwhelming desire for name recognition . . . brutal competition . . . Nobel Prize lust . . ." (Djerassi, 1997). (A pointed rebuttal to Djerassi appeared soon after [Frank, 1997].) Life for students is different, too. Scott Russell Sanders (1999) appeals to faculty to combat what he calls the culture of despair. Sanders addresses the culture of undergraduate education, where the seeds of Djerassi's competitive consumer mentality may be sown early. There is little time to acknowledge moral values in intellectual pursuit. Even the idea that we in higher education could be serving some larger good, as Sanders concludes, seems a quaint 1960s anachronism. Small wonder that national programs and professional organizations have been spending time and effort on topics such as revitalizing undergraduate education, mentoring, and examining the nature of graduate education itself.

A rich literature on mentoring exists (for example, Noe, 1988; Schaverien and Cosgrove, 1997; Krockover, 1991; Tallitsch, 1996; and Broome, 1996), including programs and recommendations for the particular needs of women (Hartman, 1995) and members of underrepresented ethnic groups (Juarez, 1991). By far, one of the most comprehensive publications on mentoring is *Adviser, Teacher, Role Model, and Friend* (National Academy of Sciences, 1997). It is a guide to assist mentors and advisers in understanding how they might help students identify and respond to the challenges of becoming scientists or engineers. It summarizes features that are common to successful mentoring relationships. The chapters define mentoring, explain the different roles the mentor plays with students (faculty adviser, career adviser, skills consultant, and role model), makes recommendations for improving the quality of mentoring, and provides resources.

The mentor-mentee relationship in scientific research is honored and time-tested, though learning to conduct research when our colleges and universities were first established differed greatly from the formal system of scholarly development we know today. The idea of a professional identity based on one's training is still valid today. Chemical genealogy is a real way that chemists record their historical connection via a lineage of Ph.D. mentors (Rocke and Ihde, 1979; McCarty, 1969; Bartow, 1939; Graham, 1948). In writing about the profound influences upon us of spending four years in a chemistry research group, a colleague and I eventually recognized that we also attribute a number of our teaching behaviors to lessons we learned from our graduate adviser (Coppola and Pearson, 1998). Somewhat ironically, and also significantly, our adviser had rarely been an instructor for an undergraduate course. The lessons have been extrapolated from his example as a mentor who valued the purpose of graduate "school" as an educational environment for the scholarly development of graduate students rather than primarily as a vehicle to advance his career. Instructional lessons emerged from the consistency of our educational experiences. We learned by example. This is a fundamental piece of understanding about mentoring: decisions we make and actions we take are all lessons we provide in our roles as advisers, teachers, role models, and friends.

A General Framework for Guiding Undergraduate Student Development

In 1994, Stephanie J. Bird identified three overlooked aspects of professional development in science students: mentoring, ethics, and professional responsibility (Bird, 1994). These three aspects cut across the traditional dimensions of faculty scholarship, namely research, teaching, and service. Undergraduate students relate to faculty in three discrete roles: students as members of a research community, students as members (even temporarily) of a professional scientific program, and students as participants in higher education. The diversity of instructional needs and objectives creates a familiar tension in formal education between training students in the technical content of the disciplines and the more overarching liberal arts values. Such values describe some *general intellectual* objectives for education. *Professional intellectual* objectives are the overarching values for a more specific literacy at the disciplinary level (for example, "chemistry," "biology," or "science"). Instructors need to attend explicitly to the connection between the professional and general intellectual objectives, namely, to answer how learning science is connected to a liberal education. Last, individual courses are embedded within the richness of *professional technical* objectives, that is, the factual subject matter that typically is comprised in a written syllabus or table of contents. Technological progress in the disciplines and the detailed articulation of the professional technical subject matter should be exploited in order to make clear connections about how learning triple integrals or translating Goethe is not only representative of professional intellectual objectives, but also addresses general intellectual ones. The implied $3 \times 3 \times 3$ grid defines an interesting space in which to examine educational recommendations:

Triad 1: mentoring/ethics/(professional responsibility)
Triad 2: research/teaching/service
Triad 3: (general intellectual goals)/(professional intellectual goals)/(professional technical goals)

Many recommendations have been nicely summarized in the references, and these will not be recapitulated here (see Bird, 1994; Broome, 1996; Juarez, 1991; Krockover, 1991; National Academy of Sciences, 1997; and Noe, 1988). Instead, this chapter will reflect the author's work within the general framework implied above.

Beginning in 1989, the University of Michigan Department of Chemistry instituted a comprehensive change to its undergraduate curriculum. Details about the start of this program can be found elsewhere (Ege, Coppola, and Lawton, 1997; Coppola, Ege, and Lawton, 1997; Coppola and Daniels, 1996b). The strategies that have been used to create a culture of sustained reform that continues to this day are intertwined with practice, but they can be summarized. In particular, our strategies are (1) to treat good teaching as transcendent because when it is done well it seeks inclusiveness for all groups; (2) to explicitly identify and articulate goals as a kind of "informed consent" for students; (3) to link these goals with actual practices, which generally requires challenging behavioral changes: the intellectual "skill" must be accompanied by the affective "will" (Paris, Lipson, and Wixson, 1983; McKeachie, 1994); (4) to recognize that, like it or not, instruction transmits values that go beyond simple lessons about the subject matter; (5) to offer multiple entry points for different learning styles, and to encourage and support all students to move beyond their learning comfort zones; (6) to make the implicit explicit; (7) to encourage living-learning communities that help students integrate their academic and social development in college; and (8) to promote group work as productive along many dimensions, and provide collaborative activities that allow for individual accountability within a cooperative framework.

Many of these strategies overlap with recommendations for gender-equitable and multicultural mentoring. Women and other marginalized communities, who perhaps fall away or simply turn away faster than others, report a consistent and "depressing discouragement" (Manis, Thomas, Sloat, and Davis, 1989) with the nature of their science experiences, including the implied messages they receive from the faculty (Seymour and Hewitt, 1997). To paraphrase Seyhan N. Ege, a colleague at the University of Michigan: "What's bad for the canary is bad for the miner." In other words, what constitutes a bad interaction for only a few is also likely to be bad for a much higher fraction. These warnings should not be underestimated or ignored.

A recent public service announcement on mentoring suggested that to be a mentor you do not have to have all of the answers, you just have to be yourself. Taken together, the strategies and ideas suggested above and in the references converge on understanding and using rational human values when you are responsible for guiding the development of another individual. The NAS monograph (National Academy of Sciences, 1997) suggests three main areas of responsibility for mentoring. Mentors build respect (take others seriously, do not dictate, are frank and direct, guide with options, encourage all opinions, take fears seriously). Mentors encourage risk and independence while providing support (recognize that ability is not the same as aptitude, and must also be flavored by ambition; strike a balance between being flexible, permissive, and restrictive; put others first when it benefits their interests). Mentors build a trusting relationship (practice what you profess; reveal yourself and your decision-making; resist the temptations of power; listen to understand, looking beneath the surface of issues to understand motivation; encourage and reflect on feedback).

Ultimately, mentoring is not an activity that can be turned on and off at will. Faculty members are mentors through all of their words and actions when they take on the public trust of education. Mentors directly influence how the next generation of mentors will behave. Another colleague on campus, Ralph Williams, uses the wonderful phrase "full human presence" to describe the combined professional and personal obligations of a faculty member to the responsibilities of guiding the development of students. "Full human presence" represents an ideal. It charges us to be honest and fully realized people in our interactions with those whom we mentor and educate. Ultimately, "full human presence" may be a particularly poignant idea in mentoring and educating undergraduate science students because the research literature indicates such a strong disidentification of young people from the scientists they see (Seymour and Hewitt, 1997; Seymour, 1992; Tobias, 1992).

Listening to the Student Voice

In preparation for writing this article, the following informal e-mail survey was distributed to the forty undergraduate chemistry and biochemistry research students being supported on summer fellowships at The University of Michigan. Eleven of these students were from other colleges and universities, and were participating in an NSF-sponsored Research Experiences for Undergraduates (REU) Site.

> Please send me e-mail replies . . . short or long, snippets or full sentences . . . on your experiences being a mentee in the following three circumstances. These may be positive or negative experiences (for some of you, they might even be about me!). You do not have to name names, and I will not reveal or connect your identity with any particular story.
>
> 1. Comment on your mentee experiences as an undergraduate research student. What has been done well or poorly as you have learned about life as a laboratory scientist? (Area label = Undergraduate Research)
> 2. Comment on your mentee experiences as an undergraduate science major. This could extend from particular events in your science courses to your interaction with faculty about science in general. (Area label = Science Major)
> 3. Comment on your mentee experiences as a college or university student. It is easy to overlook the fact that your development as a learner is also part of your higher education. Comment specifically about role models and their actions that you think have been influential on you. (Area label = University Student)

Seventeen students (43 percent, three of eleven from the REU program) replied. Individual items in each of the three areas were first categorized as being a positive or negative comment and then subcategorized according to the mentoring ideals from the prior section (related to showing respect, being supportive, or promoting a trusting relationship). Representative items in the Undergraduate Research area are provided here as an example.

Area: Undergraduate Research (positive; in other words, cited as a positive, supporting characteristic)

Showing respect: "I feel like part of the lab and not just a mentee"
Being supportive: "having to do the work myself, after nudging in the right direction"
Promoting trust: "telling personal stories about graduate school"

Area: Undergraduate Research (negative; in other words, cited as a deficiency)

Showing respect: "sometimes it was difficult to disagree with more experienced people"
Being supportive: "too little supervision: I am not always sure if I am doing the proper thing"
Promoting trust: "entering the research lifestyle was intimidating due to mentor's standards"

The numerical summary across all three categories is shown in Table 7.1.

Based on this snapshot, the three categories (respect, support, and trust) easily account for the 154 comments made by these seventeen students. By and large, these students have been in positive mentoring relationships (113, or 73 percent, of the comments describe positive interactions). Nearly all of the comments reflect the general principles found in the literature, such as "mentor takes time to talk about work, answer questions," "I learned about life," "being honest," "setting behavior by example: to work hard, and to love the work," "weekly meetings to report and brainstorm,"

Table 7.1. Summary of Survey Results

Area (number of replies)	Respect (pos/neg)	Support (pos/neg)	Trust (pos/neg)
Undergraduate Research (68 replies)	16 pos/3 neg (19/68 = 28%)	18 pos/9 neg (40%)	21 pos/1 neg (32%)
Science Major (61)	11 pos/6 neg (28%)	8 pos/7 neg (24%)	18 pos/11 neg (48%)
University Student (25)	1 pos/2 neg (12%)	11 pos/1 neg (48%)	9 pos/1 neg (40%)

"free to explore ideas . . . within limits," "realistic (neither filled me with idealistic dreams nor scared me)," "left me with determination," "telling personal stories about personal activities," "putting a human feel on the science topics," "more inclined to like advisers when they know my background and interests," "answers questions, does not talk down to me but treats me as an equal who just has more learning to do," "patient," and "I admire mentors for seemingly natural actions, rather than actions manipulated to leave positive impressions." The implied context for the negative comments are also aligned with the main topics: "sometimes being watched too closely and not getting a chance to learn through errors," "I have not felt like a mentee," "I have had professors who did not seem to care about undergraduates," "not interested in pursuing the relationship if faculty intimidate," "professors preoccupied with their status," "lab work made too routine by instructors who provided answers too quickly, even shortcuts," "the more you talk to your TA or instructor, the better the grade . . . this outraged me, so I did things on my own," and "faculty interaction is good, but it needs to go beyond posting office hours and then scolding if students do not attend them."

The relatively even distribution of comments in the research and general science area may be an indication of how robust these categories are for describing mentoring. Not surprisingly, the students are not as reflective about their general university education as they are about the more specific programmatic areas; this is an indication of student life in the dis-integrated university. The range of reasons offered by this sample of students reflects the value of full human presence in the classroom. Recently, The University of Michigan has been developing low-enrollment general-education seminars for first- and second-year students, as well as capstone courses. The discourse on our campus about these plans is centered on providing more reflective courses in the "liberal arts tradition" for our students. The results from this small survey are congruent with this need.

Program Examples That Support Mentoring

In this section, some of the specific courses and programs implemented by the author are described as models for the reader. These activities draw explicitly from the mentoring framework outlined above. Again, a few new directions for teaching and learning will be suggested here in lieu of recapitulating published work.

Developing the Scholarship of Teaching and Learning: Chemical Sciences at the Interface of Education. Graduate and postgraduate concerns about mentoring in science have focused on the next generation of scientists in their capacity as researchers. This target needs to be broadened without sacrificing the benefits to research, which means becoming more efficient at what we do. For over a decade, the Carnegie Foundation for the

Advancement of Teaching has advocated a broader understanding of scholarship and its relationship to faculty work. In *Scholarship Reconsidered,* Ernest Boyer (1990) reminds us that scholarship is a mode of thought and a way of practice that can be applied to all aspects of faculty work.

Inasmuch as *Scholarship Reconsidered* provides a broadened answer to the question, What is scholarship?, its follow-up, *Scholarship Assessed,* answers the next implicit question, What tools do we use to distinguish the more scholarly from the less scholarly? (Glassick, Huber, and Maeroff, 1997). In the strength of its persuasive argument, *Scholarship Assessed* also provokes a new question, and that is, How does scholarship arise? If research is not the exclusive domain of scholarship, then understanding how we develop our research scholarship becomes a model for how we develop scholarship in general. Scholarship arises through a deliberately constructed infrastructure of professional development in which mentoring relationships play a large role. Through formal and informal work, undergraduates are identified for their scholarly potential and, in the majority of institutions today, provided with opportunities for increasing autonomy and responsibility through independent study and research. These same principles apply to graduate students, with some variation in the balance between formal course requirements, tasks such as proposals and seminars, and research. Research has become the focus of scholarship, and scholarship's infrastructure has become synonymous with the development of research skills. This development continues through the postdoctoral level and provides a momentum for a faculty member's professional career.

What would it look like to broaden the infrastructure of professional development to include the broadened notion of scholarship? In my work, I have been creating the pieces of the infrastructure that are devoted to the scholarship of teaching, beginning at the undergraduate level and extending to the faculty level. CSIE: Chemical Sciences at the Interface of Education (http://www.umich.edu/~csie) is a project devoted to creating and documenting exemplars within the professional development infrastructure that supports the scholarship of teaching in chemistry. We are exploring undergraduate curriculum design that allows students to have a mentored experience in examining their potential for teaching. Junior and senior students can move into more independent work in design, implementation, and assessment. In the graduate program, first-year chemistry Ph.D. students can take their cognate courses in education science or educational psychology and then work with experienced faculty in designing, implementing, and assessing curriculum ideas in our department. As in the department's research program, graduate students will soon play a significant role in the teaching program. In their third and fourth years, these students participate in weeklong mentored teaching internships at nearby institutions that are quite unlike our own. The next stages of this work are under way, where I am working with different disciplines at my own campus and with chemists at other institutions. We have also modeled work with postdoctoral students.

Eventually, a multidisciplinary, multicampus network of institutions is needed so students can actually move through a system.

The CSIE argument underlies some recent recommendations for improving precollege education. At the end of "Some Features of a Flawed Educational System," an article in *Daedalus,* Seymour Sarason (1998) points out that blaming teachers for the inadequacies of education is blaming "the well-meaning victims of an educational system that they did not design." Ken Wilson and Constance Barsky, in the same issue, propose that only by studying and understanding the success of continuous change in our existing "sociotechnological systems" will we be able to bring lasting reform to education (Wilson and Barsky, 1998). They conclude that education is the system most in need of learning from applied research and development. Until we provide mentoring for a broadened notion of scholarship, we will not break free from repeating cycles of reinventing reform in each generation. What we call curriculum reform is more often than not faculty reeducation because the informed professional development of faculty for instruction is lacking. Larry Cuban asserts that the process of reform is itself unexamined (Cuban, 1990). In his essay, "Reforming Again, Again, and Again," Cuban concludes that "waves [of reform] occur on the surface [of formal education] and, in some instances, programs, like the skeletons of long-dead sea animals, get deposited on the coral reef of schooling . . . [yet reform itself goes critically unexamined]. . . . I end with a plea for rationality . . . If we do not heed the plea, we will continue to mindlessly speculate, and as Gide observed, 'Everything has been said before, but since nobody listens, we have to keep going back and begin again'" (p. 4).

Structured Study Groups. In our Structured Study Group (SSG) program, a cohort of 120 first-year students within the 1200-student Structure and Reactivity chemistry course (standard coursework and examinations) earns honors credit by participating in extra weekly two-hour sessions (Coppola and Daniels, 1996a). This supplemental instruction is shaped, metaphorically, along the lines of a performance studio in the arts. Assignments, in the form of common (not identical!) tasks, are subjected to peer presentation and peer critique facilitated by upper-level undergraduate leaders. Students in the structured study groups follow a detailed curriculum that helps them develop the kinds of skills that we believe are attached to a deep mastery of the subject matter in a format that encourages the students to also develop their more general learning skills, including their ability to work and communicate within the large, diverse setting of our institution.

During each session, the meeting time is typically divided between a number of activities. Each participant brings a duplicate set of his or her written assignments from the previous week. These assignments generally involve the creation of examples within a given context. In the first assignment, they pick a molecule from a chemistry journal (after learning, in their session, how to decode line formulas, what journals are, where they are found, and what a proper citation format is) and are directed to construct five rational examples of molecules with the same formula. They then propose rankings for their created molecules based on three of six chemical or physical properties. They must also include written descriptions of their rationales. Later, a typical assignment might be to find an example of a representative reaction in a chemistry journal and format it as a quiz problem appropriate to the level of the class. At the beginning of the session, each student submits one copy of his or her work to the peer group leader, and the other copy is distributed to the class. One or two rounds of peer review follow. The reviewer does not correct the other student's paper, but rather answers a set of factual questions about the other's work using an assessment sheet as guidance. During this time, the discussion within the group is freewheeling, and it is the time of greatest learning for the students. It also builds a strong sense of peer community, drawing from ideas such as respect, support, and trust, as these students share work with each other with the idea of productive critique. The first round of peer review can take up to an hour. Only when faced with reviewing the work of another can students deal with issues that were either incorrectly understood or that simply did not occur to them. After a second round of reviewing is completed, the reviews and the unmarked papers are returned to the originator and he or she has a chance to decide if any corrections are needed. This set of assignments and reviews are collected, and they form part of the basis for the leader's evaluation of the student's performance on that day.

Each term of the course in which structured study groups are used ends with a project that lasts a few weeks. In the first-term course, the students receive copies of two or three journal articles, usually short communications, in which chemistry appropriate to the experience of the students can be found. For three weeks, along with their last sets of assignments, the students create and edit a set of questions that might be asked of the author (usually one of our chemistry colleagues). During the last week of classes, the entire cohort of study group students meets with the author, who then fields the questions asked by the students. These sessions are quite powerful in their impact on the members of the class, who report wholesale shifts in their identities from "first-term chemistry students" to "members of a valid scientific discussion." Admittedly, we have taken a page from our colleagues in English, who, for example, routinely arrange meetings between students and the author of a piece that the class has been studying. The SSG curriculum covers a range of important topics. For example, we introduce formal ethical reasoning related to scientific practice (Coppola and Smith, 1996; Kovac, 1996; Kovac, 1999; Coppola, 2000). To end the second semester course, the students spend the last three weeks creating, refining, and peer editing their own case studies in scientific and professional ethics. Analyzing ethics cases is one of the tasks in the first term, too. In a separate section of the second-term course, students have a number of term-long projects, including generation of the text (in traditional print, HTML, and CD-ROM involving animations and other dynamic correlations) on which their final examination is based. More information about the SSGs can be found at http://www.umich.edu/~michchem/SSG (copies of the curricula for both terms and student-leader resources can be requested from the author).

The benefits of the SSG experience are not limited to its participants. Juniors and seniors, who are the group leaders, identify those participants who demonstrate potential for teaching excellence as the next generation of group leaders. This transition is the beginning of the professional development infrastructure described in the last section. From the beginning, SSG leaders have been collaborators on the design and delivery of the SSG program. Weekly sessions with the SSG leaders are informal, collaborative seminars on teaching and learning. The following quote is from one of my undergraduate teaching mentees, who had just completed his junior undergraduate year, in 1997. It is representative of a 1994–95 first-year student who demonstrated potential for teaching while participating in the SSG program, and someone who the CSIE program could more formally develop once he entered the junior year. He worked on independent teaching projects with me for three years, and on independent research with one of my colleagues. Before he left for graduate school, he and I had collaboratively designed, implemented, and assessed a curriculum project that in every way exceeds even the best independent study research project I have collaborated on with an undergraduate student. He writes, "The most important lesson I learned was that the 'teacher' is never just an instructor, but a student as well for the rest of their life. This became evident after going through the program first as a student and then as an instructor. . . . I believe that my students taught me as much as I taught them, so I also had the opportunity to be a student myself. No matter how long a person has been involved with classroom instruction, I believe that they will always have things to learn if they allow it. A person never graduates from being a student, as there are always people that can teach them. This was an experience that I will never forget. It was an experience that made me realize my love for teaching chemistry. I hope that I will always be able to teach in a classroom, and I hope that I won't forget that I will always be a student."

A Professional Development Capstone Course in the Chemical Sciences. At the end of the undergraduate curriculum, the department of chemistry has recently instituted a capstone course called Professional Development in the Chemical Sciences. The course is constructed around the variety of modes of expression that can characterize a life in science: written and oral, from short and long technical reports for various professional audiences to communicating with the public. The students in this course, nearly all of whom have participated in undergraduate research, once again revisit case studies in research ethics from the perspective of more experienced scientists. The majority of these students go on to graduate school or employment in chemical industry, so there is a strong practical component to this discussion.

The "professional development" aspect of training chemical scientists includes but is not limited to research ethics. Over the past decade, perhaps partly as a result of the increasing number of cases of unprofessional and unethical practices, we recognize that unspoken and implicit instruction is clearly inadequate for the many practical and behavioral expectations of a life in science. As both academic and industrial scientists, we acknowledge the need to be more proactive in explicitly addressing the "rules of the game" of professional citizenship. Nationally, there is a groundswell of interest in how we introduce future scientists to the complex and challenging choices they must learn to make in their professional lives. Not only is the widely practiced "trial and error" method an unimaginably inefficient strategy, but the occurrence and consequences of professional malpractice are disturbingly high.

Some professional development issues occur naturally during the regular administration of courses, especially laboratory courses, and certainly in research, where issues in data and time management, "authorship," and responsible behavior are encountered daily. On the other hand, formal discussion can become too decontextualized or limited to putative response after a problem has already occurred. By creating a broad-based course, we provide an opportunity to reveal some of the complexities of a professional life in science in a way that will allow students a relatively safe and supervised environment. We have been influenced greatly by our industrial colleagues who report that their new employees, while adequately trained for the technical aspects of their work, have little professional experience where communication within a complex political and social structure is necessary. One of the 1999 research students who responded to the survey about mentoring is spending the summer interning at a nearby pharmaceutical research laboratory. As a student, he was a loner who actually disdained interaction with others because he wanted to prove something to himself about his independence. His advice to instructors after just a few weeks of his internship is telling: "I suggest that even though someone is keeping to himself or herself and does well, the instructor might want to intervene. I have learned through working in industry that it is really important to interact with those around you."

Student Organizations. The collective memory of the work of undergraduate student clubs is often fleeting, perhaps even more so than the memory of some academic faculty committees! Unlike fraternal organizations, with which members still identify long after they leave their student years, undergraduate students in preprofessional clubs more naturally disidentify with their organizations once they graduate and are no longer undergraduates. In addition, these clubs generally lack externally mandated local or national structures and so they end up tied strongly to their idiosyncratic institutional setting. As the faculty adviser for both the Alpha Chi Sigma chemistry fraternity and the American Chemical Society Student

Affiliates (ACS-SA) at my institution, I have observed the relative consistency of the former group and the periodic peaks and troughs of the latter.

Like some of its earlier successful incarnations, the 1997–98 ("peak") group of ACS-SA at the University of Michigan owed a great deal to the individual students who came in on a "trough" and revived the program. Unlike with earlier incarnations, though, I have worked with these students to create some proactive strategies with which they hope to establish a structure and a tradition that will permit the organization to survive after the innovators have graduated. In this way, their problem is the same one we face in curriculum development: how to get innovations to survive the innovator so that we do not end up having to reform "again and again" (Cuban, 1990).

The work of these student affiliates contains lessons about allowing newcomers to take ownership, about cooperation and compromise, and about simple enthusiasm and love for the subject. Another strategy is contact and communication in a larger forum, so members of the group can more effectively learn from each other's experiences. Strategically, setting up a professional organizational structure has worked well. As an adviser, I am more of a collaborator with professional experience in the organization. My only requirement for the students is that they share ideas and strategies with me before enacting them. Similar to the case studies in research ethics that they study, I also ask them to examine explicitly the impact on stakeholders and the breadth of other issues related to their plans. I urge them to explore the things they can do within that limitation, and I support them in the independent efforts they undertake, including organizing over eight presentations and three peer-reviewed publications for which I am appropriately not a coauthor. Ironically, national American Chemical Society program officers have inserted my name on the author list for some of the presentations done by the ACS-SA. This example also illustrates that the main NAS areas (respect, support, and trust) work well to guide mentoring practices.

One-on-One Mentoring via the World Wide Web. By now, we are all accustomed to the benefits of electronic communication in bridging the distance between faculty members and undergraduate students. Those students who seek you out via electronic mail are not just the ones who visit you after class or at your office. The new medium opens new opportunities to a group from whom you might not have otherwise heard. Even when the invitation is open and repeated, what inspires a student to finally communicate with you? Using a personal Web site is another way to begin a mentoring opportunity.

Faculty Responsibility and Moral Obligations

Mentoring involves ideas and behaviors. When it comes to faculty behaviors, we have already made the point that the current mode of professional development falls short of its needs. Faculty members use their own graduate experiences and participate easily in meaningful conversations, and often-productive debates, about their research. Mentoring and teaching are an implicit part of the faculty contract. Yet conversations about these topics are limited and uninformed. Outside of schools of education, university faculty members are notorious for their disdain of pedagogy. We all know research scholars who seem to feel that knowledge of content is all that matters, and that attention to issues beyond this somehow dilutes or demeans the hard-earned value of subject-matter knowledge. If we provide a good course, full of the latest developments in our field, students will learn. We focus on teaching rather than learning, often with disastrous results. Lunch table conversations about current courses are often filled with destructive nostalgia about how much better students were "in the old days." Facilitating a broad-scale conversation about pedagogy is a difficult task, particularly in a university where faculty are engaged significantly in research, but a morally reflective educational practice (which is a type of content) demands that pedagogy be taken as seriously as factual content. At least in the public eye, students are the reason for the existence of the university. Their interests in a high-quality education that prepares them to be effective participants in the society are paramount. We must move beyond the views that (1) teaching is merely the organization and delivery of content, and (2) the primary goal of pedagogical innovation is the production of "artifacts" such as textbooks or, currently, interactive computer programs and Web sites. Pedagogical innovation requires changes in faculty behavior, the most difficult change of all. It is the difference between knowing (intellectually) that a good diet and regular program of exercise are truly the right things to do and observing that the world has plenty of overweight, sedentary physicians who also smoke. Behavioral changes are more complex and difficult than just changing one's mind. Because they require a change at the core, the process is slow. The first step is to facilitate a public discussion of pedagogy among university faculty, initially at the department level, eventually broadening so that ideas can be shared across disciplines. This is mentoring, too.

As heretical as it may sound, we can learn a great deal from the moral development of our medical school colleagues when it comes to how we "treat" our students: this above all else—first, do no harm. We have all observed first-hand (or perhaps simply heard from authoritative sources) too many examples of teaching and mentoring behaviors that we should never permit. These are uncomplicated issues of right and wrong. If we remain silent when we see or hear of these incidents then we are as guilty of abandoning our responsibilities as are the perpetrators. We fail as mentors. If we demonstrate our hypocrisy with "do as I say, not as I do" then we are as guilty as they. Mentors need to practice what they profess. We must have the moral courage to simply go to our intellectual offspring and say "no, what you are doing is wrong" instead of meeting behind closed doors and making whatever decision about these individuals fits our local custom.

"First, do no harm" is not a prescript of inaction. It is a glaring reminder that our students have come to us for our care: for us to provide them with a rich environment in which they can improve themselves. If our students need our treatment, then we must diagnose carefully and wisely. On the day we earn our Ph.D. degrees, we faculty should be much better educated about the obligations of our profession. This is an obligation of mentoring. If we, by our words and actions, do not know how to provide the kinds of interventions that permit the majority of students to improve themselves, including every member of the next generation of faculty, then we may be guilty of negligence at best . . . and more often of actual harm. Ignorance is not an excuse. Full, open discourse about the scholarships of teaching and service and their inclusion in the professional development program for new faculty is the most morally defensible viewpoint for improving the state of teaching and learning.

References

Bartow, V. "Chemical Genealogy." *Journal of Chemical Education*, 1939, *16*, 236.

Bird, S. J. "Overlooked Aspects in the Education of Science Professionals: Mentoring, Ethics, and Professional Responsibility." *Journal of Science Education and Technology*, 1994, *3*, 49–55.

Boyer, E. L. *Scholarship Reconsidered: Priorities of the Professoriate*. Princeton, N.J.: Carnegie Foundation for the Advancement of Teaching, 1990.

Broome, T. "The Heroic Mentorship" *Science Communication*, 1996, *17*, 398–429.

Coppola, B. P. "Targeting Entry Points for Ethics in Chemistry Teaching and Learning." *Journal of Chemical Education* 2000, *77*, 1506–1511.

Coppola, B. P. and Daniels, D. S. "The Role of Written and Verbal Expression in Learning. Promoting and Improving Communication Skills for Students in an Undergraduate Chemistry Program." *Language and Learning across the Disciplines*, 1996a, *1*(3), 67–86.

Coppola, B. P., and Daniels, D. S. "Structuring the Liberal (Arts) Education in Chemistry," *Chemical Educator,* 1996b, *1*(2), S 1430–4171(96)02018–3. Available at http://journals.springer-ny.com/chedr.

Coppola, B. P., and Daniels, D. S. "Mea Culpa: Formal Education and the Dis-Integrated World" Science *and Education*, 1998, *7*, 31–48.

Coppola, B. P., and Pearson, W. H. "Heretical Thoughts II. These on Lessons We Learned from our Graduate Advisor That Have Impacted on our Undergraduate Teaching." *Journal of College Science Teaching*, 1998, *27*, 416–421.

Coppola, B. P., and Smith, D. H. "A Case for Ethics." *Journal of Chemical Education*, 1996, *73*, 33–34.

Coppola, B. P., Ege, S. N., and Lawton, R. G. "The University of Michigan Undergraduate Chemistry Curriculum. 2. Instructional Strategies and Assessment," *Journal of Chemical Education*, 1997, *74*, 84–94.

Cuban, L. "Reforming Again, Again, and Again." *Educational Researcher,* 1990, *19*, 3–13.

Djerassi, C. Letter to the Editor. *Chemical & Engineering News*, August 18, 1997, 8.

Ege, S. N., Coppola, B. P., and Lawton, R. G. "The University of Michigan Undergraduate Chemistry Curriculum. 1. Philosophy, Curriculum, and the Nature of Change," *Journal of Chemical Education*, 1997, *74*, 74–83.

Frank, P. Letter to the Editor. *Chemical & Engineering News*, September 8, 1997, 6.

Glassick, C. E., Huber, M T., and Maeroff, G. I. *Scholarship Assessed: Evaluation of the Professoriate*. San Francisco: Jossey-Bass, 1997.

Graham, R. P. "The Genealogy of a Chemistry Department." *Journal of Chemical Education*, 1948, 25, 632.

Hartman, I. S. "AIM: Attracting Women into Sciences." *Journal of Chemical Education*, 1995, 72, 711–713.

Juarez, C. E. "Recruiting Minority Students for Academic Careers: The Role of Graduate Student and Faculty Mentors." *Political Science and Politics*, 1991, 24, 539–540.

Kovac, J. "Scientific Ethics in Chemical Education." *Journal of Chemical Education*, 1996, 73, 926–928.

Kovac, J. "Professional Ethics in the College and University Science Curriculum" *Science & Education*, 1999, 8, 309–319.

Krockover, G. R. "Reflections on Professorial Mentorships." *Teaching Education*, 1991, 3(2), 113–114.

Manis, J. D., Thomas, N. G., Sloat, B. F., and Davis, C.S.G. "Factors Affecting Choices of Majors in Science, Mathematics and Engineering at the University of Michigan." *Center for the Education of Women Research Report*. Ann Arbor, MI: Center for the Education of Women, 1989.

McCarty, C. N. "Chemical Genealogy." *Journal of Chemical Education*, 1969, 46, 317.

McKeachie, W. J. *Teaching Tips* (9th Ed.). Boston: Heath, 1994.

National Academy of Sciences. "Adviser, Teacher, Role Model, and Friend: On Being a Mentor to Students in Science and Engineering." Washington, D.C.: National Academy Press, 1997. Available at http://www.nap.edu/readingroom/books/mentor (viewed July 2, 1999).

Noe, R. A. "An Investigation of the Determinants of Successful Assigned Mentoring." *Personnel Psychology*, 1988, 41, 457–479.

Paris, S. G., Lipson, M. Y., and Wixson, K. "Becoming a Strategic Reader." *Contemporary Educational Psychology*, 1983, 8, 293–316.

Rocke, A. J., and Ihde, A. J. "A Badger Chemist Genealogy: The Faculty at the University of Wisconsin-Madison." *Journal of Chemical Education*, 1979, 56, 93.

Sanders, S. R. "Teaching Thoughtful Students the Rudiments of Hope," *The Chronicle of Higher Education*, Apr. 9, 1999, XLV(31), B4–B5.

Sarason, S. "Some Features of a Flawed Educational System," *Daedalus*, 1998, 127(4), 1–12.

Schaverien, L., and Cosgrove, M. "Learning to Teach Generatively: Mentor-Supported Professional Development and Research in Technology-and-Science." *Journal of the Learning Sciences*, 1997, 6, 317–346.

Seymour, E. "'The Problem Iceberg' in Science, Mathematics, and Engineering Education: Student Explanations for High Attrition Rates." *Journal of College Science Teaching*, 1992, 21, 230–232.

Seymour, E., and Hewitt, N. M. "Talking About Leaving: Why Undergraduates Leave the Sciences." Boulder, Colo.: Westview Press, 1997.

Tallitsch, R. B. "It's Time for a Change in the Way We Educate Physiology Ph.D. Candidates." *Advances in Physiology Education*, 1996, 16, S68–S70.

Tobias, S. "Women in Science—Women and Science." *Journal of College Science Teaching*, 1992, 21, 276–278.

Wilson, K., and Barsky, C. "Applied Research and Development: Support for Continuing Improvement in Education." *Daedalus*, 1998, 127(4), 233–258.

BRIAN P. COPPOLA *is an associate professor of chemistry at The University of Michigan, Ann Arbor. He is a faculty associate at The University of Michigan Center for Research on Learning and Teaching, and a Pew Scholar in the Carnegie Fellows program of the Carnegie Foundation for the Advancement of Teaching and Learning. He directs the Chemical Sciences at the Interface of Edu-*

cation program at The University of Michigan, which is devoted to creating and documenting exemplars within the professional development infrastructure needed to understand and promote the scholarship of teaching and learning. His area of instructional research interest is curriculum design, implementation and evaluation that are mediated by multidisciplinary collaboration between faculty in chemistry, education, and psychology.

8

Drawing from teaching and administrative experiences, this chapter outlines mentoring opportunities to help students succeed in their undergraduate years and prepare for life in an increasingly diverse society.

Promoting Understanding of Diversity Through Mentoring Undergraduate Students

Margaret Scisney-Matlock, John Matlock

During the past decade, higher education institutions throughout the United States have placed considerable emphasis on increasing their numbers of minority and underrepresented students, improving racial climates on campuses, and addressing retention and graduation issues which generally tend to be lower for these students than for majority students. At the same time, colleges and universities have made significant efforts to demonstrate that diversity learning and teaching benefits all students who are being prepared for an increasingly diverse world and workplace. As institutions seek to deal with these multiple, and often complex, challenges, many faculty have had to examine their assumptions and roles relative to a multicultural campus and how they interact with students of color, as well as communicate the importance of diversity to all their students.

Furthermore, there is heightened interest in the role of mentoring within institutions of higher education as related to enhancing multicultural awareness in all students. Numerous essays, articles, and research studies have offered broad interpretations on the importance of relationships between faculty and students who come from diverse communities throughout the world. Most seem to conclude that for students to benefit from mentoring that can result in greater retention and graduation rates, as well as enhanced satisfaction with their campus experiences, the interactions between the faculty and students must be comprehensive and yet specific enough to address the social, academic, and personal development needs of students (Astin, 1993; Pascarella, Terenzini, and Hibel, 1978; Tinto, 1993).

NEW DIRECTIONS FOR TEACHING AND LEARNING, no. 85, Spring 2001 © Jossey-Bass, a Wiley company

These authors stress the importance of faculty involvement in the overall success of students in general and in most cases authors allude also to the impact on underrepresented students.

This chapter will explore some of the issues and challenges connected with mentoring students of color and the significant role that faculty have in working with this growing population—both inside and outside of the classroom—in promoting diversity learning and teaching. It will offer suggestions on how faculty can examine and challenge their own assumptions regarding perceptions of diversity and the impact they have on all students, especially students of color. Finally, practical strategies will be offered that faculty can use to encourage mentees to "think out of the box" regarding diversity. In this way, issues of diversity can often be addressed through effective faculty mentoring of students. Student comments used throughout the chapter are from undergraduates who participated in a comprehensive and longitudinal study on the impact of campus diversity during their four years in college (University of Michigan, 1999).

Defining Mentoring and Diversity Concepts as a Faculty Member

As discussed in many chapters of this book, effective mentoring can have a powerful impact on students during the time that they are in college and also when they enter graduate or professional school, or the workforce. Often, students' overall success will be influenced significantly by the impact of the mentoring relationships with faculty. Additionally, how students gain skills in interacting with others who are different in some way will be influenced by the messages given to them by faculty.

Depending on the institutional type, many undergraduates arrive on campus with very little understanding of students who might be significantly dissimilar based on racial and ethnic differences, as well as those with religious and geographic diversity (for example, international students). While they might have a willingness to establish relationships with various students, they do bring images or stereotypes of others that are not based on actual experiences or interactions. For example, a student might not have had any substantial interactions with minority students but has developed impressions based on the media, limited interactions, and what they have been told by parents and others in their communities.

This poses many challenges and barriers for undergraduates, particularly when we consider the large number who are young (eighteen- to nineteen-years old) and have limited life experience. For example, in a study conducted at a large higher-education institution, nearly 90 percent of entering white undergraduate students attended nearly all-white high schools and lived in all-white communities (University of Michigan, 1999). At the same time, nearly half of the African American students came from nearly all African American communities, and this was true of their high school as well. Students are often mixed together and expected to "work things out" relative to how they relate to each other. As one student commented, "diversity is pretty complicated stuff. When I arrived at my campus, they told us about the importance of diversity, but we didn't get the instructions to put it all together. I keep making a lot of mistakes relative to my interactions with others, and I don't know who to turn to for help." Often, it's the faculty who will have the most impact.

Reaching Common Ground: Faculty Mentor Perspectives on Diversity May Differ from the Students'

When the word "diversity" is used, it means different things to different faculty. Likewise, it also means different things to student mentees. It is important that one have a common understanding, not necessarily a common agreement, on what diversity means. For example, for a student of color, diversity may be perceived only in terms of race and ethnicity while someone else may see it from the perspective of race, gender, geography, sexual orientation, or religion. This is compounded by the fact that diversity or multiculturalism in the classroom generally is defined globally while it can be very specific when dealing with student populations. Therefore, a faculty member coming from a relatively homogeneous community may see the campus as very diverse while an African American or Latino student might perceive it to be not at all diverse. Or students may have preconceived views on the meaning of diversity. While this may seem unimportant, everyone tends to "play out his or her definition of diversity." In the end, considerable miscommunication can occur and ultimately damage good mentoring relationships on campus.

This understanding is important to developing good mentoring relationships because students often depend on faculty to help them work through these multiple definitions and maintain relationships with their peers who also are struggling with the transition to college. The goal is to work with all students in demonstrating that diversity is a value-added asset that uplifts all students, not only while they're on campus but throughout their life experience.

Faculty as a Valuable Resource for Students of Color

For students, faculty members represent a tremendous intellectual and experiential resource. Resourcefulness often has much to do with pointing students in the right direction and helping them find others who can facilitate their successful transition through their collegiate years. For students of color, who at times perceive the campus environment as hostile and unfriendly, barriers to their successful navigation of the system can hinder both academic performance and overall satisfaction with their experiences.

As a result, there are times when students will need a variety of mentoring relationships with different individuals including those faculty who generally have the most contact with them. A major role of faculty mentors is to guide students in identifying campus resources that can help them, optimally before problems develop.

Mentors are most successful when they can direct students to individuals and campus offices that can address particular nonacademic needs that are best handled by others. For example, establishing individual contacts with staff in the financial aid office or counseling office will provide faculty with greater tools to help students and avoid situations in which students' concerns are not handled quickly. It is even more helpful when the faculty member has relationships with individuals in that unit so that when students are referred, there is a specific individual with whom to communicate.

Additionally, it is essential that students develop multiple and varied relationships. Academic success is only one dimension of overall student success and satisfaction. A student who is away from home may find comfort with an individual who is like a "parent away from home," and this individual may not be a faculty person at all. The key point for the mentoring faculty member is to recognize these multiple aspects of mentoring and not to erect barriers that could hinder a student's development. As one student lamented, "my mentor thinks that he owns me and gets very uptight when I mention that I talked to someone about a problem, even though I knew that he couldn't help me. He made me feel like I had offended him and now I'm very uncomfortable around him. I'm thinking about switching mentors."

Expectations: Reaching Agreement

Mentoring relationships often fail for students of color because expectations are not spelled out at the outset. It is valuable to ask students to write out what their expectations are for their mentors as a way of ascertaining that "we are all on the same page." Because mentoring can mean so many different things to different individuals, it is essential that some common understanding be reached.

Some students may appreciate a "check in" call or an e-mail message while others might view this as intrusive. A common mistake for faculty is to assume that "one size fits all" or that there is a single ideal process for mentoring all students and that all students subscribe to that definition. Agreements can be reached relative to number of contacts per semester and the degree of informality for meetings. Students can be quite evasive when they want only limited contact with a mentor or adviser who has been assigned to them, and students are often not sure what is expected of them or of their mentor.

Addressing Stereotypes That Can Affect
Mentoring Relationships

One significant barrier that hinders strong communication with students of color is the racial and ethnic stereotypes that faculty often bring to the relationship. Students of color are very sensitive to perceptions that there are low expectations set for them or that individuals have preconceived notions relative to their academic performance and their abilities to "fit" in the institutional culture.

One often hears from students of color who indicate that their mentors assume they are having problems with a particular course because they are not smart and just need to study harder. Other students have mentioned that their mentor asked about their urban experience even though the student may come from a suburban community. Other examples include assumptions that all students of color come from poor families and that they are first in their family to attend college. A Native American student reported that his faculty mentor automatically assumed that he came from a reservation when actually he had never visited one.

Likewise, Asian American students may feel that they are expected to do well in mathematics and sciences or that their mentor is surprised if they have an interest in majoring in social sciences, education, or English. Faculty mentors often overlook the fact that there is no monolithic minority group and that each student of color is indeed unique in his or her own way. Interestingly, many undergraduates of various ethnicities share these perceptions based on limited precollege interactions with students from other racial and ethnic backgrounds. Faculty members can do much to eliminate these stereotypes by examining their own assumptions and attitudes and those of the students that they mentor. Faculty must never exhibit biases and behaviors that either validate negative stereotypes, no matter how unintentional, or reinforce those that other students might harbor.

At times, it is essential that faculty mentors step outside their own space to interrelate with students on their "own turf." Organizations of students of color often are responsible for bringing various speakers to campus, but faculty are often noticeably not in attendance. A mentor should always look for opportunities to learn from students, which means taking advantage of interactions beyond the classroom and structured environments such as the faculty member's office.

Students of color often complain that students and faculty alike ignore the fact that there is tremendous variation within different racial and ethnic groups. For example, there are more than thirty ethnic groups included in the Asian American category. Likewise, Hispanic-Latino groups come from significantly different geographic areas of the Western Hemisphere. Because of the richness of diversity within and among various ethnic and racial groups, faculty must make every effort to ensure that stereotypes don't filter into their perceptions of students of color, which can present significant barriers in interactions with their mentees.

Finally, students bring multiple identities to campus and may often shift among them. A student of color who is female, for example, may place greater emphasis on gender issues than race or ethnicity and could be very resentful that her faculty mentor views everything from a racial perspective. As one student suggested, "my adviser is one dimensional. Because he has been to Africa, he thinks that he knows everything about African Americans. I have never been to Africa so I don't know what he's talking about. My first trip abroad will be to South America." It is essential to maintain an open mind, view each student as a unique individual and remember that the word "minority" has a broad definition that contains many, many groups. There is a richness of variation between and among the different racial and ethnic groups.

Common Misconceptions Associated with Mentoring Students of Color

Within the higher-education community, discussion often centers on whether faculty of color make the best mentors for students of color. Proponents of diversification of faculty often make this case while others suggest that any faculty member should be able to mentor a student of color. The appropriate match really depends on the situation and the motives of the various individuals. The most important factor is that students of color who have a faculty mentor perform better academically, regardless of the race or ethnicity of the faculty member. The body of research suggests that one significant characteristic of students who are not performing well academically is that they did not have a faculty mentor whom they perceived as essential to their development.

In effect, these students are navigating through the higher-educational system by themselves and have disengaged from the process of developing and refining relationships with faculty. Additionally, some nonmajority faculty use this as an excuse not to work with minority students by suggesting that they might be better served by having a matched race or ethnicity mentor. This poses several problems. Students are keenly aware when they are being put off or pushed away and have difficulty accepting this rationale. Furthermore, the notion erroneously assumes that it is the responsibility of faculty of color to mentor all students of color, which overlooks the fact that many predominantly white institutions have a paucity of minority faculty. It is the responsibility of all faculty to mentor all students, regardless of race or ethnicity. Finally, these feelings can easily cause a student to feel marginalized and invalidated at a critical time in their lives. One often hears students of color expressing the feeling that they don't belong at their institution, and they often cite their relationships with faculty.

Maintaining Trust in Mentoring Relationships

Students of color, when discussing relationships with faculty who differ in race or ethnicity, often indicate that they had high expectations only to have some incident shatter their trust in the individual. For example, one student indicated that he checked with his adviser on a regular basis and thought that they had a good and satisfying relationship. However, after being told that he was doing well in his course work and that his progress was on target, he was called in to the minority affairs office only to be told that his adviser had indicated that he wasn't doing as well as he had expected. "I had never been so hurt in my life and never went to see that faculty member again. Now I'm suspicious of all faculty." It takes time to build trust relationships with students, which may be fragile at best. It only takes one incident for students to become distrustful and seek another mentor or, if they remain with their current one, to have minimal if any contact with that individual. Another student of color said that she had discovered her mentor was saying negative things about her. Before learning this, she had asked for several letters of recommendation, and was told by her adviser that she would be "more than happy to do one." Later the student found that the mentor was providing comments that had a negative impact on her in the job search. "If she had problems with me, I wish that she had told me instead of leading me to believe that all was well. I can never trust her again." These examples stress the need for mentors to be up-front with student-of-color mentees at all times, no matter how painful or difficult the discussion.

Walking the Talk: Setting the Example in the Classroom

Faculty need to know that students, especially students of color, are very aware of perceived inconsistencies that can interfere with mentoring relationships and can potentially erect walls of misunderstanding and miscommunication. For example, a student related that while his mentor is really nice and very helpful, he was concerned that in the classroom his mentor makes subtle disparaging remarks about women and minorities. "I'm not sure how to take this. If he truly was supportive of minorities, he would be more sensitive in the classroom." This student also added that during discussions about racial issues in the class, his mentor seemed to take sides with the white students. Another student commented about his mentor's research grants, stating that all the students who work with him are white. "I even indicated that I needed a job and he directed me to other offices when I knew that he was trying to fill several student positions." Another student suggested that his mentor treated students of color in the classroom as if they didn't exist, not recognizing them while they have their hands up but calling on them unexpectedly to respond to questions or asking them to give the minority point of view. These behaviors create tensions in the classroom. Mentors have to "walk the talk." Otherwise, students of color begin to doubt the sincerity of the mentor.

Establishing Good Relationships with Student Affairs Units

Much has been written about the differences in higher education between offices of academic affairs and student affairs. Often, the two key areas disagree philosophically about approaches to student development. While there have been improvements recently in drawing the two units together, much more needs to be done. The argument was made nearly a decade ago that the visible commitment to diversity seems largely to come from the office of student affairs with little involvement by the academic enterprise. Yet these are not mutually exclusive because student development issues certainly can have an impact on academic performance. For example, students who are having adjustment, financial aid, and housing problems will invariably experience difficulty academically and vice versa. Among African American, Latino or Hispanic, and Native American students, many come to their respective institutions with concerns about finances, and these concerns remain constant throughout the undergraduate years. Another illustration would be students of color who work longer hours than other students would, often while taking a full load at residential colleges. These students often have justifiable concerns about paying off tuition and related costs. Faculty mentors have to be cognizant of these issues and explore ways to get assistance for students. Academic problems may be rooted in other nonacademic issues. The mentor must have good contacts in other units of the campus including offices in student affairs that may have staff who specialize in resolving these problems.

When the Mentor-Mentee Relationships Aren't Working

When mentoring relationships just don't work well, there is a tendency to personalize situations between the mentor and mentee. It is important for all parties to try to determine the nature of the problem and how it can be resolved. Given the responsibilities of a faculty mentor, a greater involvement must be assumed by that individual. Efforts should be made to contact the student and have a frank discussion. However, it should not be a forced discussion. Students are often reluctant to discuss some issues with their mentor or with anyone else, including peers.

It may be necessary for faculty to facilitate their student's transition to another mentor, either in a formal or informal relationship. Perhaps the student has identified needs and the faculty knows some other individual more able to address them. For example, a student may want to have a mentoring relationship with someone whose academic field is connected with the student's goals. Additionally, it is wise, even when a student has ceased to be involved with a mentor, for the mentor to communicate via telephone or e-mail to see how the student is doing and to offer continuing assistance if needed. Climate perceptions are one of the major areas that appear to have an impact on the success of students of color, particularly in academic areas in relationships with faculty. Continued communication will often influence these perceptions to be positive.

Role of Academic Administration in Mentoring and Diversity Activities

Academic administrators including deans, department chairs, and academic support persons can play a significant role in ensuring that there is a supportive climate for students of color. For example, they must monitor how students are assigned to formal mentors, provide training programs for faculty mentors, and make strong statements about the importance of diversity initiatives. Administrators must be sure that there are no institutional barriers that hinder academic success. This often involves support for retention activities to address the graduation rates for students of color, which generally lag far behind those of majority students.

Strong support of student organizations, including those that are focused around minority students, sends important messages and also provides opportunities for collaborative efforts. For example, some student organizations are involved in recruiting, retention, and peer mentorship programs, but often their home departments have little contact with them and provide little support. Additionally, academic administrators must be cognizant of mentoring inequities if junior minority faculty are asked to help all students of color or are expected both to mentor individuals and to serve as advisers to student organizations. These practices not only perpetuate a system with unfairness to the faculty of color (expectations not required of others) but they jeopardize tenure and promotion opportunities as well.

Concluding Comments

This chapter has attempted to bring together several perspectives on diversity and mentoring. In a society that stresses differences and uniqueness, undergraduates, regardless of race and ethnicity, are remarkably similar in their goals, aspirations, and desire to be successful. Yet students often see the world differently based on the experiences that they bring with them to their respective campuses. Diversity and multiculturalism are areas in which students often differ in their initial perceptions. Diversity also plays an important role on campus because students have different experiences throughout their four years. Often, though not necessarily always, student campus experiences are affected by race, ethnicity, and gender. Higher education is a microcosm of society at large, and many of the significant issues involving social justice, diversity, and merit are at work on the campus. At the same time, all students are struggling with transitions from high school to college and are entering unfamiliar environments with multiple identity concerns. It is often faculty that, through formal and informal mentoring, have the opportunity to assist students in navigating through the educational system.

Faculty are key players in the development of students. Diversity is a crucial social element of life in the twenty-first century, and campuses are the place where students have the opportunity to explore the future with their mentors. The prominent emphasis on multiculturalism and diversity has resulted in faculty having to examine their own previous assumptions and consider how they interact with the increasingly diverse populations of students. In the process, diversity itself provides opportunities for both students and faculty to learn and to have an impact on one another.

References

Astin, A. W. "Diversity and Multiculturalism: How Are Students Affected?" *Change,* 1993, 25(2), 44–49.

Pascarella, E., Terenzini, P, and Hibel, J. *Journal of Higher Education,* 1978, *49*(5), 450–463.

Tinto, V. *Leaving College: Rethinking the Causes and Cures of Student Attrition* (2nd ed.). Chicago: University of Chicago Press, 1993.

University of Michigan, Office of Academic Multicultural Initiatives. *The Michigan Student Study.* Matlock, J. and Gurin, G. (principal investigators). Ann Arbor, Michigan, 1999.

MARGARET SCISNEY-MATLOCK is associate professor in the School of Nursing at the University of Michigan and also directs a faculty project exploring strategies for training faculty in multicultural learning and teaching techniques.

JOHN MATLOCK is assistant provost in the Office of the Provost, executive vice president for academic affairs, and director of the Office of Academic Multicultural Initiatives at the University of Michigan. He has done extensive research on the impact of institutional diversity initiatives on undergraduate students during their four years in college.

9

Colleges and schools of business administration can exploit the focus on improving learning outcomes by developing strategies to increase knowledge about learning, protocols for faculty to use as mentors, and relationships with actual business practitioners.

Educating the Practitioner: Strategies for Focusing on the Student in the Undergraduate Business Curriculum

E. R. Melander

Teaching as mentoring is useful in gaining an understanding of some profound shifts occurring today in higher education. For a variety of reasons, the instructional focus of institutions is becoming student-centered, moving from the presenter to the learner, from presentation to learning, from instructor ratings to learner outcomes. This shift is occurring rapidly and widely. In particular, for colleges offering programs where graduates are targeted toward professional practice, these changes point to new roles for faculty and students and new strategies for the design of learning experiences and environments.

There are new and demanding expectations being placed on higher education, and, simultaneously, there are new technologies and new understandings of the learning process to draw upon as institutions resight their visions and reconfigure their resources in support of the learner and improved learning outcomes. Students entering the world of practice must not only "know about" but also must be able "to do." They must learn to apply and so "create" knowledge, to solve problems, and to make decisions. They also must be able to do these things in settings where collaboration within and among groups is the mode of operation. They must be able to grow in their leadership capacities and in their ability to form reasoned and sound judgments. This requires sensitivity toward and understanding of differences among people and societal institutions and of the different perspectives and methodologies of many disciplines within the institution.

An institution becomes learner-centered when it places its primary emphasis on improving learning outcomes. For example, a learner-centered ideology designs and monitors the effectiveness of its curriculum, processes, services, and facilities to support learners. It also assigns responsibilities and holds agencies and organizations within the institution accountable for continuing improvement in their support of learning outcomes. Focusing on the learner and learning outcomes becomes a perspective that not only alters the roles of faculty and students, but places new expectations and responsibilities on other players and facilities that contribute to the learning enterprise of the institution. Classroom layouts, communication media and connections, group learning spaces, and access to information, knowledge, and learning systems—all may need to be reconfigured and extended. Academic administrators must adopt strategies to transform facilities and increase services that support faculty and engage student learning.

Most important, learner-centered institutions must adopt strategies that allow them to *learn* about learners, their goals and motivations and learning characteristics and processes. They must also learn more about the arenas beyond college where students will deploy and further develop their education. Within the context of available new technologies, learner development under the mentoring of the faculty is likely to become more individualized. Learner-centered institutions need to develop more powerful protocols that customize learning to the needs and styles of individuals.

The Learning Process as Learner Development

The intensified institutional focus on the learner has naturally focused attention on the learning process and the responsibilities of both instructors and learners. The role of the teacher is being reframed with new perspectives and new responsibilities. The teacher must now address questions of "how" students learn as well as "what" is to be learned and must aim toward developing learner capacities for constructing and applying knowledge.

Activities of the learner are expanded beyond traditional "listening and reading" and learner responsibilities are extended to include "active engagement" in the learning process. Measures of learning outcomes such as "recitation and reproduction" are being replaced by greater expectations of "demonstrated understanding and capacities for application in practice."

Learning is a knowledge-development process—in other words, a process promoting growth in the capacities of the learner to assimilate and accommodate received knowledge, and also to apply, organize, and synthesize knowledge. Deep learning takes place when students add to or reorganize their own cognitive structures. Superficial learning occurs when rote skills are employed to absorb and recite received bodies of knowledge. Deeper learning is transformational and empowering for the learner. The goal here is to develop learner capacities to the point where the learner is able to construct and apply knowledge in future situations without coaching.

As summarized by Ewell (1997), research has identified several keys in the learning process: the learner creates his or her learning actively and uniquely; learning is about making meaning for each individual by establishing and reworking patterns, relationships, and connections; direct experiences decisively shape individual understanding; learning occurs best in the context of a compelling "presented problem," in other words, specific, identifiable problems that students want to solve and that are within their capacity to do so; learning requires reflection; and learning occurs best in a cultural context that provides both enjoyable interaction and substantial support.

The learner is a practitioner of scholarship. The learner should be aiming at becoming operational as a scholar, in other words, developing the habits of mind and mastering of disciplines employed by scholars. Four stages in learner development are described in Table 9.1, along with examples of learning activities and experiences typical of each stage.

To foster the development of the learner, the task of the instructor becomes one of facilitator, of providing learning exercises and experiences in

Table 9.1. Learner Development Stages

	Assimilating Base of Received Knowledge	Becoming Operational in Knowledge Building	Developing and Applying Knowledge	Organizing Knowledge
Examples of Learning Activities	Memorizing categories and significant information of knowledge structures	Practicing process of creating and modifying knowledge	Assessing problem contexts and designing solutions	Formulating understanding and judgments
Examples of Learning Experiences	Reading texts, outlining concepts and context descriptions, following solution steps in problem examples, becoming information literate	Participating in exercises demonstrating concepts, practicing with tools of analysis, collaborating in establishing and conducting learning agenda	Open-ended search and discover problems, collaboration in establishing and applying criteria, assessing learning outcomes	Describing, interpreting, criticizing, instructing, mentoring

88 BEYOND TEACHING TO MENTORING

a context that promotes student growth through the stages of learner development. The instructor accomplishes this by

- *Preparing* the learner to access and engage received bodies of knowledge
- *Exposing* the learner to models of scholarship and providing practice experiences on how to construct and apply knowledge
- *Pacing* the learner through exercises leading to the mastery of scholarship skills
- *Providing* exercises that cause the learner to develop skills of assessment, interpretation, criticism, and judgment ["Managing Faculty Assets . . . ," 1999]

Effects of the Learner-Development Focus on the Role of the Instructor

With the metaphor for the learning process becoming "learning as developing through experiences," the role of the instructor moves from that of presenting a predefined body of knowledge—through lecturing and demonstrations—toward that of engaging the student in developmental activities.

Faculty have long been representatives of their disciplines on campus, concentrating both on expanding discipline boundaries and methodologies and on introducing students to the mysteries of discipline knowledge and the powers of application. Teaching as mentoring shifts faculty attention to questions of how to cause students as individuals to take on responsibilities for their own learning and how to coach them to grow in their capacities for assimilating, developing, applying, and organizing knowledge. The teacher must learn to mentor along the full spectrum of learning.

At different stages of the learner-development process, the mentor applies different strategies and undertakes different roles in managing the experiences of the learner (see Table 9.2). Early stages of learner development call for introducing students to sources of knowledge and exposing them to discipline approaches for constructing knowledge. Here, the mentor serves as a director, connector, and motivator. Soon the learner becomes ready to begin working with models and the mentor now serves as a coach, guide, or tutor. With more mature learners who are developing and applying knowledge, the role of related faculty becomes that of coach, critic, and counselor. Later learner development involves working with applications of knowledge in applied, practical settings to inform understanding and the judgment-making process. The mentor engages the student in dialoguing, reflecting, and consulting roles. Strategies are needed to help faculty understand and excel in these newer roles of learner development that typically have not been part of their disciplinary training.

Teaching as mentoring signals shifts in the focus of roles for all principals in the learning enterprise. Mentoring becomes an operational maxim for all "principals" engaging the learner within the learner-centered institu-

Table 9.2. Mentoring Students Through Learner Development Stages

	Assimilating Base of Received Knowledge	Becoming Operational in Knowledge Building	Developing and Applying Knowledge	Organizing Knowledge
Mentoring Strategies	Build learner capacities for information searching and concept recognition, identify paths for accessing knowledge and expertise	Expose learner to models of scholarship and provide practice in applying models in realistic settings	Develop learner capacities for deepening, broadening, and validating own knowledge base; construct open-ended scenarios for examining real world settings and developing problem solutions	Develop reflective practitioner capabilities, assign tasks requiring collaborative interpretation and setting of action agendas
Mentoring Activities	Directing, Connecting, Motivating	Modeling, Guiding, Tutoring	Coaching, Critiquing, Counseling	Dialoguing, Reflecting, Consulting

tion. In addition to students and faculty, other academic professionals within the institution—librarians, instructional and learning technology and system specialists, advisers, and personal-development counselors—are principals in defining the learning environment and experiences of students. Beyond the institution, practitioners who are "doing it" can become part of the adjunct faculty cadre engaging students in the learning development process. It takes a "whole village" of learning specialists inside and outside of the institution to educate a business practitioner. All serve as mentors in engaging the student in learning development activities.

Developing Reflective Practitioners in Administration and Management

Mentoring involves the strategies and practices of teachers to develop capacities of individual students to function as self-directed learners. In professional settings—for example, education for business administration—this is modified to place the knowledge and the learner in a particular context and to emphasize applications of knowledge to guide practice. Of special interest here are strategies of value to schools and colleges of business in fostering the education of practitioners.

Teaching as mentoring must address the joint goals of developing the student as a learner—someone who is going to be learning over a lifetime—

and as a practitioner—someone who will be applying specialized knowledge and skills in particular settings and will need to continue developing leadership, creativity, and problem-solving capacities in the worlds of commerce, industry, and government. This is a large and complicated task.

Many colleges of business administration are undergoing change toward transforming themselves into having learner-centered values and modes—though perhaps too slowly and without an overarching vision. Leadership is needed to identify ways of shifting the perspective of faculty and support agencies. More needs to be known about learning itself and about the relationships between learning and the learning environment. Institutional capacities for gathering and interpreting data about learning and for placing results in the hands of faculty and administrators to improve programs and processes need to be strengthened. Faculty and all other mentors in the institution need to develop "a sense of collective accountability for learning of the same character and depth as is currently accorded scholarly research." They need to develop and apply "learning scholarship" attitudes and protocols.

Strategies focusing on the student in the business curriculum translate to approaches for placing the learner in active roles in settings that reflect environments they will operate in as business practitioners (see Table 9.3). Again from Ewell, certain approaches facilitate learning. It is desirable for faculty to constructively model the learning process, for learning experiences to emphasize applications, for learning exercises to link established concepts to new situations, for learning to occur via interpersonal collaboration, for the learner to be provided rich and frequent feedback on performance, and for a curricula to be designed as integrated "learning plans" (Ewell, 1997).

An Example: Transformation of Smeal College of Business Administration Junior Core

The Smeal College at The Pennsylvania State University established faculty teams to transform its business curriculum. The goal was to introduce students to business the way it really works. They came up with a trademarked solution labeled "the Cube," for "Curriculum for Undergraduate Business Education" (see note following the References for further information).

A series of integrated courses for the junior year were developed to introduce students to basic principles of business disciplines—finance, marketing, logistics, and management, for example—and the way they work together in practice. Faculty members teach in teams and are supported by learning technologies. Business cases involving real corporations are addressed in ways that allow students to see how marketing decisions have an impact on financial decisions, and how those in turn may influence accounting and other issues. Students work on projects in teams just as they will as managers. And they learn in environments using electronic tools and systems just as they will in their professional careers.

Students no longer meet in large auditoriums to be lectured at and take rote memory tests. Rather, for example in a course addressing the manage-

Table 9.3. Mentoring Students for Functioning in Business Settings

	Assimilating Base of Received Knowledge	Becoming Operational in Knowledge Building	Developing and Applying Knowledge	Organizing Knowledge
Mentoring Strategies	Build learner capacities for information searching and concept recognition, identify paths for accessing knowledge and expertise	Expose learner to models of scholarship and provide practice in applying models in realistic settings	Develop learner capacities for deepening, broadening, and validating own knowledge base; construct open-ended scenarios for examining real world settings and developing problem solutions	Develop reflective practitioner capabilities; assign tasks requiring collaborative interpretation and setting of action agendas
Business Education Practices	Integrated courses across disciplines, team-teaching, concepts presented in practice settings	Simulations in business processes, tasks assigned requiring collaboration in identifying and applying concepts and models	Case studies in real business-world scenarios, tasks requiring team development of solutions and consensus in directed actions	Tasks requiring determining criteria for assessment of models and their applications to form decisions and judgments
Learning Environment	Learning teams, collaborative computer labs, open electronic feedback testing	Learning teams, collaborative computer labs, open electronic feedback testing	Learning teams, collaborative computer labs, open electronic feedback testing	Independent study, executive seminars, internships, service learning

ment of organizations, they are divided into small teams and work together both in and out of class. They meet around computers to complete tasks and discuss questions designed to develop their knowledge of business concepts such as strategies, organizational structure, and human resources. Periodically during the semester, student teams participate in "events" in which real-life scenarios are used to test through practice. In courses in their majors beyond the junior core, students customize their learning along career interests, learning about the management of quality and technology in diverse environmental and ethical settings.

Strategies in Transforming the Education of Lifelong Learners and Practitioners

The basic overall strategy in transforming teaching to a learner-centered focus can be straightforward. The transformation of the curriculum is to be considered as an investment. Collaborative teams of faculty, students, learning specialists, and experienced practitioners are to be formed to assemble and grow knowledge about learners, learning protocols, learner technologies, and desired learning outcomes and to design their findings into the curriculum. The teams are to participate in the delivery of the transformed curriculum and be held accountable for its continuing assessment and improvement.

To implement this overall strategy, three sets of interdependent operational strategies are needed within colleges and schools of business: (a) strategies to develop knowledge about learners, (b) strategies to develop learning protocols for faculty to use as mentors, and (c) strategies to identify and strengthen relationships with academic and student development professionals and agencies within the institution as well as with actual practitioners.

Operational strategies for assembling research on learners and customized learning protocols include

- Form learning centers within the school or college to coach and guide team members in curriculum design and assessment activities
- Promote the concept of learning-centered "teaching scholarship" as the second discipline for all faculty and learning specialist team members
- Foster structured instructional experimentation and sharing of findings by faculty, in other words, "Teaching as applied scholarship."

Operational strategies for developing learning protocols and faculty as mentors include

- Promote faculty applications of relationships between teaching strategies and learner outcomes through assignments to curriculum development and delivery teams
- Tap faculty motivation—link faculty rewards with their contributions of intellectual property

Operational strategies for strengthening relationships with academic and student development professionals and agencies include

- Develop an organizational structure at the provost level that is charged by the central administration with fostering collaboration among agencies with responsibilities for faculty, learning specialists, and learning facilities needed in reaching the goal of transforming the curriculum. The collaboration must include joint responsibilities for planning, budgeting, and allocating resources in support of interagency curriculum design and development teams.
- Appoint an interagency curriculum project management group. The group is to provide leadership and oversight for collaborative teams actually designing and developing the curriculum and new learning protocols.

The group is to serve in a liaison role between collaborating teams and their respective home-agency executive administrators.

- Appoint collaborative curriculum teams for each major consisting of appropriate faculty and students as well as learning and facilities specialists and practitioners from the field. Charge the teams with specific project goals and milestones that span the design, development, delivery, and assessment of curriculum reform.

Conclusions

The imperatives are clear for moving the curriculum toward active and collaborative learning and to take advantage of the power of technologies in the delivery of learning in residence and at a distance. As institutions navigate the transition toward learner-centered curricula, faculty roles in guiding the development of learners are a central theme—after all, faculty as teachers bear the responsibility for learning in the classroom, identifying what students are to learn, and setting standards for student achievements. Stand-up classroom performances are no longer adequate bases for judging good teaching. Faculty responsibilities are being extended to guiding student learning activities through roles such as mentoring, coaching, and counseling. How these new roles for faculty are best conducted in developing autonomous, lifelong learners and practitioners of business concepts needs to be confirmed and incorporated in the design and delivery of the curriculum. To accomplish this, there needs to be extensive collaboration among learning specialists from all agencies on campus with responsibilities for the learning environment and delivery venues. The basic overall strategy recommended to move the transformation of the curriculum forward in a collaborative setting is to consider as investments the joint design and development inputs and arrange for returns on these investments to all participants. Operational strategies to implement the overall investment model approach are recommended. They address issues of how to learn about learners, how to motivate and develop faculty, and how to assemble and manage collaborative teams for the design, development, and implementation of curricula.

References

Ewell, P. T. "Organizing for Learning: A New Imperative." *AAHE Bulletin,* Dec. 1997, 3–6.
"Managing Faculty Assets to Accommodate New Realities," *NCHEMS News.* National Center for Higher Education Management Systems, Feb. 1999, 2–5.

Further Reading

Christensen, C. R., Garvin, D. A., and Sweet, A. (eds.). *Educating for Judgment: The Artistry of Discussion Leadership.* Cambridge, Mass.: Harvard Business School Press, 1991.
Dewey, J. *Experience and Education.* New York: Simon and Schuster, 1997.

Schön, D. A. *The Reflective Practitioner: How Professionals Think in Action*. New York: Basic Books, 1983.

Spence, L. "What Do We Know About Learning?" Workshop notes from the director, Schreyer Institute for Innovation in Learning, The Pennsylvania State University, Nov. 1999.

For descriptions of Smeal College of Business Administration Junior Core Courses, visit the college's site at http://www.smeal.psu.edu/smeal/thecube.html or a site maintained by the Schreyer Institute for Innovation in Learning at http://www.inov8.psu.edu /innovations/ba304.htm.

E. R. MELANDER *is faculty research associate, Center for the Study of Higher Education; professor emeritus of quantitative business analysis, Smeal College of Business Administration; and associate vice provost emeritus, undergraduate education, The Pennsylvania State University.*

10

From a careful description of the rationale and implementation of a large-enrollment, science-based, introductory class, faculty can use an interdisciplinary course model to explore specific and innovative mentoring opportunities. This model describes a hierarchical mentoring system with key roles for faculty team members, graduate students affiliated with the class, and undergraduates.

Mentoring Interdisciplinary Undergraduate Courses

Timothy L. Killeen

In this chapter, I discuss the special needs and opportunities for effective faculty and graduate-student mentoring of undergraduates in an interdisciplinary model. These undergraduates are enrolled in large science-based, interdisciplinary, introductory (SBII) courses. I derived the commentary from five years of experience as the course director for the two-semester sequence—*Introduction to Global Change, Part I: Physical Impacts* and *Part II: Human Impacts*—at the University of Michigan. Although this model is specific with regard to topic and campus location, any interdisciplinary faculty team can apply the lessons learned and possible implementation strategies.

New experiments with introductory science curricula, such as the University of Michigan's Global Change courses, are being conducted for two principal reasons. First, these courses are influential in determining students' career and academic choices, often providing the final opportunity for certain students to gain a basic appreciation for science and the scientific method as part of their general education. Second, past assessments in many disciplines have shown that students can sometimes be permanently alienated from science by traditional courses that emphasize rote learning. In response to these concerns, extensive efforts were made during the past decade to reform introductory curricula in mathematics (Artique, 1999), chemistry (Lloyd, 1994), physics (*Physics Education Research,* 1999), biology (Coalition for Education in the Life Sciences, 1999), and other disciplines, as well as to develop new interdisciplinary courses, designed to be broadly accessible to and appealing for first-year students. The mentoring in these classes is a key source of motivation for students to continue to study science.

New Directions for Teaching and Learning, no. 85, Spring 2001 © Jossey-Bass, a Wiley company

As a unique mentoring option, interdisciplinary courses for introductory science-based curricula are no longer as novel a concept as they were in the early 1990s, but the effective implementation of such SBII courses, and their evaluation in terms of student learning, represents a significant challenge and opportunity for undergraduate educational reform. The large enrollments in these courses mean that direct, one-on-one, faculty-student mentoring will be constrained by the practical considerations of limited faculty time. Therefore, other mentoring techniques (the hierarchical model) must be used to help all students reach enhanced levels of more active and collaborative learning. In some sense, the initial development and continuous improvement of these important large-enrollment courses demand the "wholesaling" of techniques that have proved successful in smaller, more intimate settings, where direct faculty mentoring is possible.

In this chapter, I describe how the University of Michigan Global Change introductory course sequence has been adjusted to improve student learning and to raise student levels of interest in science through use of mentoring by faculty and graduate student instructors (GSIs), the implementation of active learning strategies, the deployment of new instructional technologies, and the use of feedback derived from extensive formative and summative assessments.

Background and Motivation

The need for effective science, mathematics, engineering and technology (SME&T) teaching at the introductory undergraduate level is one of great import and scale. Consider that, in the U.S. postsecondary educational system alone, there are roughly 14 million students enrolled in 3,600 institutions, and these students earn 1.9 million degrees per year (about 1.4 million are granted in nonscience and engineering areas). These students (both science and nonscience majors) are the teachers, legislators, industrial decision-makers and researchers of tomorrow. All of these students will need a working background and knowledge of science to confront the complex challenges of an increasingly technological society in a world of limited natural resources (Clinton and Gore, 1994).

It is clear that we cannot afford a postsecondary educational system that "turns off" students from even a rudimentary appreciation for scientific thought and quantitative analysis. Yet, there are alarming indications that show that's exactly what is happening. At the K–12 levels, for example, the findings of the Third International Mathematics and Science Study (TIMSS) provide cause for concern. These findings were reviewed by the U.S. National Science Board (NSB) which subsequently issued the call to arms, "Failing Our Children, Implications of the Third International Science and Mathematics Study"(National Science Board, 1998). The TIMSS report showed that only one quarter of U.S. high school students enroll in physics and only one half in chemistry. In a later and more complete analysis of the TIMSS data, the NSB developed recommendations for needed reforms in instructional materials, teacher preparation, college admission strategies, and evaluation and assessment research (National Science Foundation, 1999).

At the undergraduate level, there are similar indicators of a systemic failure to capture the interest of students who are not (at least initially) inherently motivated to study SME&T topics. A study in 1995 indicated that fewer than 20 percent of students take an SME&T course after their freshman and sophomore year. College attrition rates are very high. Of the 2.4 million students entering four-year colleges in 1993, 1.1 million left without a degree. The graduation statistics are lower for specific underrepresented groups, such as Hispanics, who graduate at a rate of 35 percent, and African Americans, who graduate at a rate of 45 percent (Tinto, 1993). Regarding science education, disturbing facts are often heard. Some surveys of Americans indicate, for example, that less than 50 percent of adults know that the Earth orbits the Sun once per year and that only one person in fifty was able to describe the scientific process, accurately, as one that is based on a process of observation and hypothesis testing. The central concern here, of course, is that fewer and fewer citizens are comfortable with the concepts of science and technology at a time of greatly expanded societal reliance on such tools. This is a concern that must be shared among all faculty and administrators in higher education.

The recent report of the National Science Foundation entitled, "Shaping the Future: New Expectations for Undergraduate Education in Science, Mathematics, Engineering and Technology"(National Science Foundation, 1996), and Volume II of that document, published in 1998 (National Science Foundation, 1998) point to specific reforms to address these problems. The central recommendation from these reports is to better integrate research and education and provide more active learning opportunities for all students, regardless of background. In other words, students will become motivated and will learn if the materials are presented in a manner that is interesting and *engaging*. There is general consensus and much evidence that effective mentoring techniques are central to such reform. The mentoring is an essential element of the motivation to continue to study science.

The Undergraduate Research Opportunities Program (UROP) Model

The past decade has, in fact, seen numerous successful reforms, designed to link research and education and enhance faculty-student mentoring at undergraduate institutions. Many universities, for example, have adopted the Undergraduate Research Opportunities Program (or UROP) model. UROP matches undergraduate students with individual faculty members, thereby enabling the students to conduct authentic research and scholarly activity in research labs, libraries, and studios. Results from published evaluations of such programs indicate that they lead to improved student outcomes in the critical metrics of both retention and scholastic achievement. The University of Michigan's UROP, which involves more than nine hundred students annually, for example, has been carefully evaluated with a process involving equivalently qualified control groups. The University of Michigan UROP includes a peer advising group component, as well as the core faculty-student research partnership, such that mentoring occurs at both the peer and faculty levels. An evaluation of the University of Michigan UROP (Nagda, Gregerman, Jonides, von Hippel, and Lerner, 1998) has demonstrated that retention rates rise for most categories of students. For example, underrepresented minority participants in UROP, studied from 1989 to 1994 had an attrition rate of 11.4 percent compared to 23.5 percent for nonparticipants. While still in their infancy, such systematic evaluations generally support the extensive positive anecdotal evidence familiar to most individuals involved in such one-on-one mentoring programs.

Table 10.1 summarizes some of the UROP intervention strategies and the student outcomes tied to these strategies, as determined from the UROP assessment work. It is generally accepted that the effectiveness of UROP is attributable, at least in part, to the intensive mentoring received by program participants at different levels—by faculty, by other members of faculty-led teams (for example, graduate students and postdocs), and by peer groups. The feeling of being welcomed on a large campus, of making useful contributions to research, and of the enhanced collegiality associated with a more intimate relationship with faculty are all key components.

Table 10.1. Elements of Mentoring Success Exemplified Within UROP Programs

Element	Student Outcome Facilitated
One-on-one faculty mentoring	Academic competency
	Critical thinking
	Academic integration
	Enhanced retention
Feeling of being welcomed on campus	Participation in learning communities
Peer group advising	Connections between classroom theories and concepts
Research participation	Computer literacy
	Teamwork
	Substantive reading
	Hands-on activities
	Logistics and problem-solving skills
Learning skills and career development workshops	Computer database management, library research in the information age, exploring the Internet, abstract writing, and time management
Annual Symposia	Oral and poster presentation skills

There remains a challenge of scale, however, and it is one exemplified by the University of Michigan situation. The 900 UROP students are a relatively small fraction of the 23,500 undergraduates enrolled in classes. Consider first an essential question. How can the positive attributes of UROP-like programs be distilled and incorporated "wholesale" into the standard curriculum? In this context, the introductory, interdisciplinary course is a relatively new curriculum tool that has significant potential. Consider also a more-focused question. What elements of successful student outcomes as seen within the UROP model (Table 10.1) can be attained within the constraints of a more traditional classroom experience?

Variety of Mentoring Strategies Available in SBII Courses

The SBII model provides mentoring options for all the faculty who are involved plus roles for graduate student instructors and undergraduates themselves.

Team Teaching. SBII courses can be developed and taught in various different ways. Typically, such courses are developed around a clear focus provided by emphasis on a theme or a collection of themes. Thus, for example, SBII courses in earth-system science are often taught with a *place-based* theme or a focus on a *resource* in question (for example, drinkable water). The courses are sometimes taught by individual professors who attempt to become sufficiently familiar with materials outside of their research area to give an interdisciplinary overview. Alternatively, SBII courses can be team taught, using expert instructors from the various intersecting disciplines, with all the challenges that this implies for overall course coherence and coordination. The latter approach is quite hard to accomplish successfully, even though the commitments on the part of individual instructional team members are smaller in magnitude than would be the burden on a single instructor. These difficulties arise because of the cultural and jargon differences between university departments, teaching styles, and even the manner in which scientific content is described across the disciplines.

The team-taught SBII course, however, has several significant potential advantages for active student learning and for an expansive mentoring approach. These advantages include (1) the exposure to diverse points of view and faculty from different parts of the university at an early date in students' undergraduate careers, (2) the possibility of institutional commitments of resources, in addition to those from the individual departments, and (3) the general enrichment of the curricular content due to access to the continually refreshed expertise of the instructors teaching in their research fields of interest.

This curricular enrichment often involves the use of instructional technologies, combining materials from the different disciplines by using multimedia and Web-based means. Additional student interest can be gained through the development of modular "case studies" of interesting topics, derived from the particular disciplinary backgrounds of instructional team members. These case studies can often be made relevant to the life interests of students, thereby engaging further involvement and appreciation for the applicability of the scientific underpinnings to matters of interest to the students.

Hierarchical Mentoring. Mentoring within an SBII course is often considered primarily in the context of graduate student instructors (GSIs), who are responsible for grading and managing lab offerings, and who often also provide student office hours for consultation. It is important to expand this thinking in the light of the powerful example of successful mentoring in UROP and other programs (Table 10.1).

The GSI is, of course, a keystone player in the student-faculty-pyramid resource and careful course design is needed to optimize the impact of graduate student participation. For example, we have found that lab sections of greater than twenty students are much less successful in terms of student mentoring than are smaller groups. This upper limit (maximum twenty students per lab section) essentially sets the institutional price for an SBII course. GSI training should include attention to the importance of mentoring in all interactions with the students. Such training should occur very early in a given term or semester to set the tone for the ensuing work. Thus, for example, the GSI-led lab section could and should be seen primarily as a mentoring experience, with graduate students fostering the development of learning communities, team building, computer, and communication skills. The term paper or team project can also be viewed explicitly as a mentoring experience, with the GSI soliciting student ideas initially, then having the students formulate the research plan more concretely in written form, and finally aiding the development and "publication" of the research project.

Teaching faculty can also participate in the mentoring of students in large-enrollment SBII classes, though this often takes the form of e-mail advice and exchanges with larger collectives of students. In a faculty team setting, the effort can be distributed by having standing agreements that designate which faculty member handles what class of query or comment. We have found that e-mail listservs are excellent resources for faculty mentoring of students. Also, faculty interactions during two-to-three-hour review sessions prior to each midterm and final exam, "movie nights," and other such activities all provide opportunities for faculty to engage with the large student group more actively outside of the classroom. Within the classroom, time can be allotted for open discussion and for questions with all faculty participants and the whole class.

Finally, undergraduate students themselves can contribute to the mentoring environment within the SBII course. We have used undergraduates as Web developers, as course coordinators, and as content developers for the University of Michigan Global Change courses (implementation through the UROP) and this has proved remarkably successful. In fact, undergraduate students who have taken the Global Change course sequence are very well positioned to advise the new group of students, providing an element of peer counseling. Also, honors student groups can improve the lab and lecture content through accelerated projects that go beyond the standard curriculum.

In summary, the design of the SBII course, GSI training and course staffing, and the course content (cadence and exposition) can all be optimized around the goal of the mentoring of the undergraduate student. In this way, the large-enrollment SBII course can mimic many of the attributes of the more intimate one-on-one mentoring afforded by UROP. Required alterations in the SBII design to make this happen, however, are not always self-evident, and a well-crafted evaluation program (including formative elements) can serve to identify and prioritize the needed modifications. These techniques are very successful in improving student attitudes towards the introductory science-based course experience.

Active Learning Strategies. The SBII course lends itself well to the development of active learning strategies. Courses with a major lab component can offer specific research activities that include the elements of teaming, oral and written presentations, hands-on research, and so on. Student groups can be formed to develop end-of-term Web posters on a topic of their choice, bringing in the important teamwork and team-building skills. The use of the Internet can facilitate student access to items such as self-tests, evaluation instruments, student portfolios, and links to other resources that provide active learning experiences. Group e-mail listservs can be used to provide electronic communication pathways for subsets of students, for student-graduate interactions within a lab section, and for the whole class, including the instructional faculty.

Institutional Reforms. Experience with the University of Michigan Global Change course has shown how valuable such a strategy can be. The optimization of an SBII course to serve the mentoring function described above requires an institutional-level commitment. It must be recognized that such courses are more (not less) expensive than other types of introductory science courses. The faculty time commitment needed to prepare and particularly to coordinate lectures is considerable, the lab sections have to be kept small to foster communication, sufficient numbers of graduate students need to be hired and trained effectively, site licenses may be needed, a special classroom may be required, and additional personnel needed. The University of Michigan Global Change course, for example, requires a "course coordinator" position, outside of the regular instructional team, to facilitate and enable the details of managing a complex educational experience (dealing with, for example, site licenses, meeting rooms, scheduling issues, curriculum committees, and so on). Also, extensive use of the Internet requires specialized expertise and a dedication to continual maintenance of the system (inactive and poorly maintained Web sites can discourage active student learning). The University of Michigan Global Change course team includes a graduate student dedicated to maintain the Internet site.

Another type of commitment from the institution might be in the form of an evaluation and assessment program. SBII courses are, by their very nature, somewhat experimental. They need to be tuned for performance, to reduce redundancy and ensure that the lab sections and lectures are properly synchronized. The best way to ensure that the curriculum meets its potential is to conduct a formative and summative evaluation program. Experience with the University of Michigan Global Change course has shown how valuable such a strategy can be.

All these components add up to a significant level of support needed from the institution. The "hero" model of a successful course, where an extraordinarily committed individual manages to inspire the students and create a masterful curriculum, is less likely to work within the constraints of an SBII course, where a larger team is necessarily involved. Successful examples of such SBII courses need to be institutionalized to ensure that the perhaps considerable institutional investment is not lost over the long term, when key instructors go on sabbatical, for example. Convincing the institution of the need to provide and sustain the commitment of such resources over time is a significant challenge that must be met if such courses are to succeed.

The University of Michigan Global Change Course Sequence Model

Experience with the Global Change course sequence has demonstrated the usefulness of multifaceted mentoring approaches within the context of a standard-format class. The Global Change course sequence has been designed specifically for nonscience majors from any school or college within the university and from any academic background. The course development has been funded by the National Science Foundation through its program the Institution-Wide Reform of Undergraduate Education (DUE–9652117). As such, the curriculum has been used as a test for reform approaches designed to provide more active, inquiry-based learning in SME&T topics for all undergraduates enrolled at a large public university.

An interdisciplinary faculty group from six departments and schools initiated the Global Change sequence in 1990. Professors involved in team teaching the course come from the Department of Atmospheric, Oceanic and Space Sciences in the College of Engineering, the Departments of Biology, Geological Sciences, and Sociology in the College of Literature, Science, and the Arts, and from the School of Natural Resources and the Environment. An independent evaluation team from the School of Education has been part of the team since the inception. After two years of planning and after arranging the necessary cross listing, the curriculum was first offered in 1992. The sequence currently involves two core courses at the 100 level, the first (offered in the fall term) deals with the physical impacts of global change and the second (offered in the winter term) deals with the human impacts. As with other courses of its type, the Global Change sequence uses Web-based tools extensively. All the lecture notes are posted on the Web (http://www.sprl.umich.edu/GCL) with each professor adopting a common format for each module, comprising objectives, readings, hyperlinks, updated text with copyright-cleared graphics and animations, a summary, and a student self-test. The course is therefore enriched by an electronic text, which is under continual revision to reflect new findings by experts in the various disciplines.

In addition, the undergraduate students develop a sense of "ownership" for the course texts by suggesting links, developing their own home pages, and team projects on the Web. Similarly, each lab is Web-based. The first semester exposes students to a dynamical modeling package, Stella™, and the second semester uses a Geographic Information System (GIS) package, ArcView™. The dynamical modeling package allows students to work directly with nonlinear complex systems to develop an improved understanding of change and causality. For example, students develop models of the earth's energy balance that are used to study global warming scenarios based on a description of atmospheric processes and projections of the buildup of carbon dioxide in the earth's atmosphere due to fossil-fuel use. Similarly, the GIS package enables students to study aspects of the global and regional utilization of resources, using a simplified version of the same tool used by governmental and nongovernmental decision-makers, such as the World Bank. These two software packages enable students to work directly with key problems in global change and examine remediation and mitigation strategies in a quantitative, hands-on manner.

A "Web poster" project is required of all students and they form teams (two to four students each) early in the term and work subsequently to develop and present their projects. Students are asked to formulate their project plan in writing, and this proposal is reviewed by the GSIs. Past experience has shown how these efforts can serve to create nested learning communities within the student body, while also providing for extensive GSI-led mentoring opportunities.

The overall goal of the Global Change curriculum project was to develop an introductory science-based course sequence that would provide *all* students, regardless of background or mathematical proclivities, an opportunity to gain the benefits and insights from a modern and continually updated scientific description of the changing global environment and the human relationship with that environment. It was felt that the issues to be discussed in such a course could be made directly relevant to the future lives of students, thereby making the content of significant appeal and interest. A key objective from the beginning was to make the course truly interdisciplinary, through a team-teaching approach, involving expert faculty from the key intersecting disciplines. The goal was to make the course both rigorous and quantitative in terms of its scientific content and still be engaging and appealing to non-science majors, through the extensive use of multimedia techniques and new instructional technologies. Both terms carry four credit hours and involve three hours of lecture and a weekly two-hour lab, together with a team project activity. The enrollment has steadily grown to the current maximum of two hundred students (primarily first year nonscience majors).

In order to assess the effectiveness of the curriculum development effort, a comprehensive evaluation plan was developed and implemented by an independent team of educational researchers not directly affiliated with the instructional team. The evaluation plan was designed to use both formative and summative perspectives to guide the development of the curriculum over both the short term (lecture to lecture and lab to lab) and the long term (year to year). One of the principles of the evaluation plan was to adopt a comprehensive and intensive approach, integral to the overall program, avoiding last-minute add-ons. Formal course objectives were articulated (Exhibit 10.1). Weekly meetings of the instructional team and the evaluation team, for example, were instituted in 1995 and have continued through to the present. A particularly valuable component of the evaluation approach has been the "minute paper" that each student is required to fill in after every laboratory exercise. Minute papers document the students' immediate response to the particular curricular element and, when reviewed over time from a statistical point of view, provide very clear guidance as to the optimal content and the cadence for the introduction of lab materials.

The Global Change team at any time typically includes four to six primary teaching faculty, five to six graduate student instructors (GSIs) drawn from various schools and colleges, a three-person evaluation team (one faculty

Exhibit 10.1. Objectives of the University of Michigan Global Change Curriculum

1. To improve students' understanding of the interdisciplinary scientific underpinnings involved in the study of Global Change.
2. To study the evolution of the physical world to enable students to better appreciate the temporal and spatial scales of changes that have occurred in the past as well as those that might occur in the future.
3. To understand why Global Change studies require a system perspective in which many interacting components must be described.
4. To become better equipped to contribute to the important debates concerning global resource management, environment, environmental impact, and societal adaptation strategies.
5. To learn to use the vast resources of the Internet to find and use environmental information.
6. To learn to develop simple dynamical models of Earth system processes and to understand the importance of computer modeling of Earth's complex physical systems as well as the limitations of their use.
7. To learn about the inadequacies in the data and knowledge regarding Global Change and to learn about emerging strategies to improve the state of our knowledge.

member and two graduate students), a student "Web-master," and several undergraduate students enrolled in the University of Michigan UROP, working on specific aspects under the supervision of one or another of the teaching faculty. This relatively large interdisciplinary team is exposed on a weekly basis to the results of the evaluation program, thus providing motivation and information to track the effectiveness of all course components. The weekly meetings provide a forum for GSI training and an opportunity for the faculty to refine the course content in the light of findings from the evaluation team. This team approach provides a hierarchical mentoring system to support the enrolled undergraduates, and much of the information gleaned from the evaluation effort has led to improvements in this mentoring process.

The course sequence was designed from the outset (1) to serve all students, regardless of level of scientific background and (2) as a coherent interdisciplinary product, using the diverse strengths of faculty at a large research university. Both of these goals were easy to articulate but quite difficult to achieve in practice.

Accessible Science for All Students. Inspired, in part, by the "Shaping the Future" document and by the goals of the NSF Institution-Wide Reform program, the introductory sequence was designed to serve all students at the University of Michigan. Figure 10.1 shows the rise in enrollment from the time of the first Web-based offering. Because the course sequence was, by its nature, interdisciplinary, it did not belong to any one school or college and this meant that academic advisers were not as likely to recommend the course to incoming first-year students. Student awareness of the course sequence was, therefore, largely developed through word of mouth and this led to a relatively slow increase in enrollment. The slow increase threatened the course sequence, and patience was needed. Currently, the course is oversubscribed and initial discussions are under way about opening a second lecture section. The course sequence also forms the basis for an interdisciplinary minor in global change, approved by the University Curriculum Committee in late 1999.

Interdisciplinarity. Although the course sequence was initially designed to be team taught, several years elapsed before the course material was actually presented in a seamless, interdisciplinary fashion. The use of a common Web format and the weekly meetings of the instructional team members were both central to this labor-intensive but critically important process of curricular refinement. All of the lectures have now been revamped to fit the Web template, providing an accessible, graphically appealing "textbook" for the course. Forcing all lecturers to conform to the same template assured continuity and integration while retaining flexibility and allowing for future evolution. A complete series of multimedia laboratory modules for Introduction to Global Change I and II has been developed using the Web site for storage, archival, and communication purposes. The Global Change curriculum features several "case studies" in

Figure 10.1. Student Enrollment in the Global Change Course Sequence

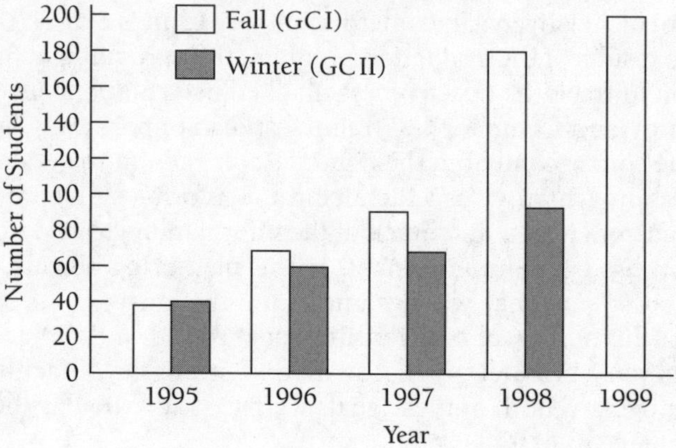

which the relevant faculty member applies his or her personal research interest to a topic in global change. Since many of the participating faculty have exciting research programs, the case studies are popular with the undergraduate students.

Mentoring. Mentoring takes place at several levels within the Global Change structure. The students are introduced to between four and six teaching faculty on the first day of classes, and these faculty are available throughout the term by e-mail and in person for student interactions. While often not available for one-on-one counseling, the teaching faculty participates in various informal meetings each term in which issues can be raised and advice sought. The term-project presentations, movie nights, exam review sessions, in-class discussions, and so on all provide additional opportunities for faculty-student interaction. The common "ownership" of the class Web page and the e-mail listserv helps to build a faculty-student relationship that goes beyond the standard lecture model.

The GSIs are very important human resources and the student-GSI relationship represents the front line of the mentoring approach in the Global Change program. Various techniques have been adopted to optimize these interactions, based on results from the evaluation program. These include limiting the size of the lab sections, reducing the cadence of computer labs and interspersing discussion sections, counseling GSIs weekly, providing a teaching manual and a day-to-day calendar for GSI activities, and using one or more experienced individuals each term to act as a group leader for the GSI team. Collectively these adjustments have greatly improved the GSI-student relationship as seen in the evaluation instrument devoted to this interface.

In general, the experience of the University of Michigan Global Change course sequence has been very encouraging. The majority of the GSI appointments are now institutionalized and the Global Change program is in the process of being expanded to develop the first interdisciplinary minor at the University of Michigan. The evaluation results (summarized at http://www-personal.umich.edu/~dey/ucdt) point to increased student engagement, learning, and satisfaction as the Global Change courses have been revised over time. The use of several instructors from different disciplines appears to contribute to students' ability to understand global change concepts, while potential transition problems have been minimized by careful coordination within the instructional team. It is believed that a significant component of the success of the Global Change sequence has been due to the emphasis placed on those elements of effective mentoring summarized in Table 10.1.

Summary

The importance of well-designed introductory science courses is generally accepted due to the significant impact that such courses can have, for good or bad, on subsequent student careers. Science-based courses can be configured to provide the kind of nurturing and mentoring environment that has proved to be successful in the more intimate formats afforded by undergraduate research opportunity's UROP. With careful evaluation, and with an appropriate level of institutional commitment, science-based, interdisciplinary, introductory courses such as the University of Michigan's Global Change sequence can indeed serve to enhance the overall student experience by providing a rich, supportive learning environment.

References

Artique, M. *The Teaching and Learning of Mathematics at the University Level: Critical Questions for Contemporary Research in Education.* Monthly Notices of the American Mathematical Society, December 1999.

Clinton, W., and Gore, A. *Science in the National Interest.* White House Policy Statement, August 1994.

Coalition for Education in the Life Sciences. *Professional Societies and the Faculty Scholar: Promoting Scholarship and Learning in the Life Sciences.* University of Wisconsin, 1999.

Lloyd, B. (ed.). *New Directions in General Chemistry.* Washington, D.C.: American Chemical Society Division of Education, 1994.

Nagda, B. A., Gregerman, S. R., Jonides, J., von Hippel, W., and Lerner, J. S. "Undergraduate Student-Faculty Research Partnerships Affect Student Retention." *Review of Higher Education,* 1998, 22(1), 55–72.

National Science Board. *Failing Our Children: Implications of the Third International Science and Mathematics Study.* Washington, D.C.: National Science Board, July 1998, NSB 98–154.

National Science Foundation. *Shaping the Future: New Expectations for Undergraduate Education in Science, Mathematics, Engineering and Technology.* Report of the Advisory Committee to the National Science Foundation's Directorate for Education and Human Resources. Washington, D.C.: National Science Foundation, 1996, NSF 96–139.

National Science Foundation. *Shaping the Future, Volume II: Perspectives on Undergraduate Education in Science, Mathematics, Engineering and Technology.* Report of the Advisory Committee to the National Science Foundation's Directorate for Education and Human Resources. Washington, D.C.: National Science Foundation, 1998, NSF 98–128.

National Science Foundation. *Preparing Our Children: Math and Science Education in the National Interest.* Washington, D.C.: National Science Foundation, Mar. 1999, NSB 99–31.

Physics Education Research: A Supplement to the American Journal of Physics, Supplement 1 to Volume 67, No. 7, July 1999.

Tinto, V. *Leaving College: Rethinking the Causes and Cures of Student Attrition.* (2d ed.). Chicago: University of Chicago Press, 1993.

TIMOTHY L. KILLEEN *was associate vice president for research and professor of atmospheric, oceanic, and space sciences in the College of Engineering at the University of Michigan until his move in May 2000 to become the director of the National Center for Atmospheric Research in Boulder, Colorado.*

11

Increasing diversity within universities, an expanding knowledge base, and new technological tools are some of the forces shaping higher education today. Models of teaching must be responsive to such developments to elevate the quality of education provided in the twenty-first century.

The Transformation of Teaching

Graham B. Spanier

The faculties in our institutions of higher education today have an unprecedented opportunity to make a difference through their teaching. The reach of this educational impact is greater than ever with the substantial rise over the last two decades in the nation's college participation rate: two-thirds of high school graduates now go on directly to college. The current economy is hungry for the higher level of analytical and communications skills that a college education promotes. Society in general is urgently in need of the inclusive worldview that higher learning helps to develop. Furthermore, the rapid changes that characterize virtually every aspect of commerce not only call for the leadership of highly educated workers, but also create a burgeoning demand for continuing higher education.

At the same time that our teaching capacity is being called upon to contribute more profoundly to human, economic, and cultural progress, our models of teaching must be transformed to accommodate varieties of developments including increasing diversity among students, an exponentially expanding knowledge base, and the ever-emerging tools of information technology. With such changes, instructional objectives are far more ambitious than in the past, seeking not to provide a fixed education, but to inspire and enable lifelong learning. Hands-on problem solving, service learning, and teamwork are among new approaches being taken to achieve this end.

As the day-to-day learning of students unfolds in such broad contexts, the faculty remains the most influential factor in educational quality. They continue to set the standards, determine the content, and deliver the necessary instruction. Yet their role as teachers is also changing in keeping with the new expectations and opportunities for learning that now exist. In addition

NEW DIRECTIONS FOR TEACHING AND LEARNING, no. 85, Spring 2001 © Jossey-Bass, a Wiley company

to "transmitter of knowledge," some new descriptors come to mind as faculty provides leadership for the learning communities of colleges and universities today: coach, facilitator, and mentor.

Diversity of Students

A transformation in the role of the faculty is in accordance with nationwide calls to rededicate higher learning to students. Among them, the Kellogg Commission on the Future of State and Land-Grant Universities urges institutions to put students first, in part by "meeting the legitimate needs of learners, wherever they are, whatever they need, wherever they need it" (Kellogg Commission, 1997, p. 9).

Students today are vastly different in demographic identifiers from those of the past and are expected to become even more diverse in the coming years. These demographic, personal, and cultural changes influence what is taught and learned in the context of formal courses and through out-of-class experiences. How faculty relates to students is also affected.

The fastest growing segment of enrollments in recent years has been adult and part-time students. The percentage of college students twenty-five years of age and older increased from 28 percent in 1970 to 43 percent in 1996; part-time enrollments grew from 32 percent to 43 percent over the same period (U.S. Department of Education, 1998, p. 198). These trends suggest that more students are bringing more extensive life experience that will filter into their higher learning.

While the concept of the student as an "empty vessel to be filled by the instructor" may never have been totally appropriate, it is absolutely obsolete for those who by virtue of their age, work, or family and community responsibilities have already accrued a great deal of knowledge. These students have a head start on many of the overarching goals of higher education. They tend to be more highly focused on their educational objectives and often have a great deal of information to contribute in class discussions that goes beyond the assigned texts and readings.

Truly effective teaching builds on the backgrounds of learners regardless of their age or experience. We have come to understand that students learn best when they can make material their own by integrating it into their existing frameworks of understanding. The broad spectrum of "previous knowledge" represented among college students today challenges faculty to get to know the members of their classes and diversify their approaches to content accordingly. Students, for their part, are challenged to assume responsibility for a more active involvement in the learning process.

Minority enrollments nationwide totaled 26 percent in 1996, compared to 16 percent two decades before (U.S. Department of Education, 1998, p. 187). This increase in racial and ethnic diversity can only be expected to continue in the future, which brings certain issues to the forefront of the attempt to accommodate the changes taking place in higher education.

Retention, for example, is a special concern for students from groups that have been historically underrepresented in higher education. Many of these students are the first generation in their families to attend college and are in need of a strong network of encouragement and support across the campus community. As the primary point of educational contact with students, faculty have a particularly important role to play in such efforts, and, more generally, in creating an environment in which all members of a diverse academic community can learn from one another. Humanizing our institutions by giving priority to such climate concerns on an individual and interpersonal level is a very important factor in the quality of education we provide and in the qualities we encourage in our graduates.

The need to be concerned about all aspects of student development is reinforced by a multitude of social and cultural changes in evidence on college campuses today. A recent summary of such developments points to changes in values, family background, and goals for young people (Hansen, 1998). Students today, for example, are less likely to say that developing a meaningful philosophy of life is an important educational objective and are more likely to look to increased earning power as the primary benefit of college. Many more are politically disengaged compared to the past. Substance abuse among youth is on the rise, with more than 40 percent of all college students engaging in high-risk behavior and binge drinking.

These are some of the indicators that tell us one of the biggest educational challenges colleges and universities face is developing character, conscience, and social responsibility in a society that often gives the impression that such virtues are optional. These are aims not readily addressed through traditional classroom teaching. They call for experiential learning and reinforcement in both academic and extracurricular settings.

One effective means of promoting student character development is involvement in community service. Service learning opportunities can be especially powerful when focused through an academic course that merges practice with theory. In such courses the experience, rather than the teacher, becomes center stage; the role of the instructor is more like a mentor who helps to identify the problems, develop and facilitate external relationships, and encourage critical analysis on the part of students.

There can be no doubt that changes in teaching are being made imperative by changes in students. Sensitivity to increasing individual differences, a broadening of educational aims, and attention to learning both in and out of classrooms are some of the emerging demands on those who carry out the teaching mission.

Growth in Knowledge

With the knowledge base now estimated to be doubling every few years, an education not only represents a shrinking sample of what might be studied but also must provide preparation for a lifetime of similar exponential change.

Our students need expert advice in choosing from among the many interests and courses that are found today across any institution and within any given field. The challenges inherent in general education provide one useful illustration. Whereas once there was a relatively circumscribed canon that all students were expected to cover, today there are many more voices and perspectives that contribute to the comprehensive worldview that reflects contemporary society—too many to be covered within the requirements for a degree. The increasing specialization within virtually every field forces choices that did not exist in the past. Students need help negotiating the options before them to achieve a coherent and satisfying educational experience. Faculty are in the best position to advise about their own fields, to promote the interdisciplinary connections that are increasingly important to understanding the complexities of the world, and to delineate educational foundations that will best serve their students' interests.

Our students also need to develop the habits and skills that will enable them to keep current with the continuing flow of new knowledge and to keep abreast, if not one step ahead, of rapid change. We must help students learn to think critically and creatively—to seek out and synthesize relevant information, to analyze from many perspectives, to draw sound conclusions, and to solve problems successfully. Proactive approaches to learning give students practice in these skills and reinforce the notion that learning never ends. Here the role of faculty is to guide students using their own personal journeys of discovery and by means of such activities as class discussions, independent projects, research experience, practicum learning, and other methods that emphasize engagement.

In addition to critical thinking and problem solving skills, the ability to work in teams is high on the list of qualities employers seek in our graduates. Collaborative learning experiences, in which students share responsibility for a project or problem, set the stage for collaboration later on in the workplace and in our communities.

The vast expansion of knowledge, the rising use of sophisticated technology in everyday life, the globalization of many societal concerns, and the continuing acceleration of all these changes have made intellectual capital the greatest resource for the future. Enabling our students to make sense of all that surrounds them is the beating heart of their higher education and the solemn responsibility of all those within our institutions who work with them.

The Impact of Technology

Advancements in information technology continue to revolutionize the efforts of students and faculty alike. The pace at which these developments are occurring is breathtaking. Even more astounding is the impact of the new digital technologies on the processes of teaching and learning. On both counts, colleges and universities no longer go about any area of their business as it was conducted just a decade ago.

New digital technologies are enabling instruction to become more inter-active. E-mail and other networking modes can increase interaction between students and teachers and among students, changing the traditional one-way flow of communication emanating from the professor that has been so much the staple of instruction in the past. Use of e-mail in college courses nation-wide increased from 8 percent in 1994 to 40 percent in 1998 (Campus Computing Project, 1998, p. 2). More frequent feedback from the instructor, increased opportunities for students to ask questions, and the facilitation of team-based projects are some of the advantages e-mail offers.

The World Wide Web, multimedia, computer-assisted tools for design and writing, and other applications all support a more active student-learning process. Realistic computer-based simulations provide practice in critical thinking and problem solving. Multimedia presentations demonstrate concepts and elaborate context, giving learners greater opportunity to engage with subject matter. The use of computer-assisted design, computer-based foreign language tutorials, word-processing software for writing and editing, and other technology tools enables repeated practice of skills and in many cases gives students experience with applications they will later be using on the job.

These developments have substantial implications for faculty. To the extent that digital resources are incorporated into a course, instructors become managers and facilitators of a variety of learning experiences and may share the role of content expert with others whose lectures or instruc-tional materials may be accessed electronically. As the tools of technology free up time that might otherwise have been spent covering content, faculty may be able to devote more of their efforts to leading discussions or work-ing with small groups or individual students. Some see the "unbundling" of teaching tasks made possible by technology as a source of cost efficiency (Young, 1997).

Indeed, with the growing opportunities for distance learning opened up by the Internet, ever-increasing numbers of students and faculty never meet face-to-face. In virtual time and space, primary responsibilities of the instructor must be to monitor and provide feedback on the progress of inde-pendent student efforts and to facilitate group communication.

The new tools of technology enable the academic community to do things that were not possible just a short time ago. They provide important means and flexibility for meeting the educational needs of students today. Yet to make the most of technology, and counteract many of the dehuman-izing aspects of on-line communication, faculty and students must redefine their understanding of instruction and acquire new skills.

Teaching in the Twenty-First Century

Our institutions need to become more learner-centered, with learning expe-riences no longer being confined to the physical limitations of classrooms. Teaching needs to be transformed into a multidimensional effort to promote and support the educational development of students.

While the faculty will continue to hold primary responsibility for teaching, this responsibility will be discharged in new ways. There will be increased opportunities for collaboration with others, and one of the most important changes will be the augmented responsibility students take in the process of teaching and learning. With these changes, faculty must take on the roles of manager, mentor, and coach with much of their "teaching" accomplished in ways that represent a marked departure from practice to date. These new roles must be encouraged and supported through special initiatives, collegial forums, and focused incentives.

At Penn State, for example, our Center for Excellence in Learning and Teaching provides programs, services, and resources designed to increase understanding of the teaching-learning process, promote teaching as a scholarly activity, and encourage interdisciplinary conversations about teaching and learning among all members of the university community. Our Learning Colloquy, convened by the provost, brings faculty together annually to discuss the enhancement of teaching. Penn State's Schreyer Institute for Innovation in Learning is a laboratory for the creation of active and collaborative learning environments. We have instituted a freshman seminar as part of the university's general education requirements to promote closer student-faculty relationships early in a Penn State education. There are several efforts in support of integrating technology in teaching and learning, including education technology services within the Center for Academic Computing.

These are just beginning steps in the transformation of teaching. Based on three years and 120 innovation projects with eighty-nine faculty members that affected some twelve thousand students, the 1998 annual report of Penn State's Schreyer Institute for Innovation in Learning concluded that the transformation of teaching is equally a transformation of learning (Schreyer Institute, 1998).

Working closely with students, faculty can create an exciting new model that will serve the future well.

References

The Campus Computing Project. "The 1998 National Survey of Information Technology in Higher Education." November, 1998. Retrieved from the World Wide Web at http://www.campuscomputing.net/summaries/1998/index/html.

Hansen, E. J. "Essential Demographics of Today's College Students." *AAHE Bulletin,* 1998, *51*(3), 3–5.

Kellogg Commission on the Future of State and Land-Grant Universities. "Returning to Our Roots: The Student Experience." Washington, DC: National Association of State Universities and Land-Grant Colleges, 1997.

Schreyer Institute for Innovation in Learning. "Annual Report." The Pennsylvania State University, 1998. Retrieved from the World Wide Web at http:www.inov8.engr.psu.edu/about/annual.htm.

U.S. Department of Education, National Center for Education Statistics. "Digest of Education Statistics, 1998." (NCES Publication No. 1999–036). Washington, DC: U.S. Government Printing Office, 1998.

Young, J. R. "Rethinking the Role of the Professor in an Age of High-Tech Tools." *The Chronicle of Higher Education,* Oct. 3, 1997, p. A26.

GRAHAM B. SPANIER is president of The Pennsylvania State University. He chairs the Kellogg Commission on the Future of State and Land-Grant Universities and the Commission on Information Technologies of the National Association of State and Land-Grant Universities.

INDEX

SBII (science-based, interdisciplinary, introductory) courses, 95, 99–102
Schaverien, L., 58
Schoem, D., 20
Scholarship Reconsidered (Boyer), 64
Schön, D., 10
Schreyer Institute for Innovation in Learning (Penn State), 114
Scisney-Matlock, M., 75, 84
Seidel, H. M., 28
Settimi, P. D., 25, 34
Seymour, E., 60, 61
"Shaping the Future: New Expectations for Undergraduate Education in Science, Mathematics, Engineering and Technology" (NSF report), 97, 105
Shulman, L. S., 10, 12, 53
Silverberg, L. A., 37
Sloat, B. F., 60
Smeal College (Penn State) "Cube" program, 90–91t
Smith, D. H., 66
Smith, K., 27
Smith, K. A., 19
"Some Features of a Flawed Educational System" (Sarason), 65
Spanier, G. B., 109, 113
SSG (Structured Study Group), 65–67
Stanford University, 51
Stid, M. A., 27
Stimmel, B., 27
Stodolsky, S. S., 9
Student character development, 111
Student engagement activities, 19–20, 86
Student Fulbright Program, 46–47
Student organizations, 68–69
Student-to-student mentoring: of engineering students, 41; by GSI (graduate student instructors), 96, 100–101
Students: benefits of liberal arts education to, 15–17; future of higher education, 17–19; learning and engagement activities by, 19–20, 86; mentored through learner-development, 88–89t; mentoring health professional, 25–33; mentoring international study by, 43–48; mentoring liberal arts, 49–55; mentoring technical discipline, 35–42; professional-professorial distinction and, 52–54; reflections on relationship of mentor and, 51–52; REU survey on mentoring experience by, 61–63; undergraduate science, 57–71. *See also* Diversity of students; Mentoring relationships
Students of color. *See* Ethnic students

Sullivan, New York Times v., 51
Superficial learning, 86–87
Tagg, J., 10
Tallitsch, R. B., 58
Teachers: developing student as learner role by, 89–90; manager metaphor for, 10–11; mentor metaphor for, 11; as performer, 9–10. *See also* Faculty; Mentors
Teaching: goals addressed by mentoring as, 89–90; linking mentoring to, 9, 12, 69–71; self-revelations on performance model in, 9–10; transformation of higher education, 109–114; transformed into learner-centered focus, 91–93
Teaching transformation: diversity of students and, 110–111; impact of technology on, 112–113; knowledge base growth and, 111–112; learner-centered focus of, 91–93; opportunities for higher education, 109–110; in the twenty-first century, 113–114
Technology: Global Change course use of, 103, 105; impact on teaching by, 112–113; mentoring use of, 69
Terenzini, P. T., 19, 75
Thayer, H. S., 27
Thomas, N. G., 60
TI (teaching intern), 41
TIMSS (Third International Mathematics and Science Study), 96
Tinto, V., 75
Tobias, S., 61
Tompkins, J., 9, 10
Trevino, F. M., 26, 27
Trust issues, 81

UCLA Higher Education Research Institute, 36
UFO (Undergraduate Fellowships Office) [Penn State]: creation of, 43–44; fostering international awareness through, 47–48; international study through, 44–45; U.S. Student Fulbright Program grants through, 46–47. *See also* International study programs
University of Manchester (England), 45
University of Michigan: Department of Chemistry, 59; diversity of students at, 76; Global Change courses, 95–96, 98–107; REU survey of, 61–63; student research experiences at, 20; UROP model used by, 98–99
University of Michigan (ACS-SA), 69

Back Issue/Subscription Order Form

Copy or detach and send to:
Jossey-Bass Inc., 350 Sansome Street, San Francisco CA 94104-1342

Call or fax toll free!
Phone 888-378-2537 6AM-5PM PST; Fax 800-605-2665

Back issues: Please send me the following issues at $23 each
(Important: please include series initials and issue number, such as TL90)

1. TL _____

_____

_____

$ _____   Total for single issues

$ _____   Shipping charges (for single issues **only;** subscriptions are exempt
from shipping charges): Up to $30, add $5^{50} • $30^{01}–$50, add $6^{50}
$50^{01}–$75, add $8 • $75^{01}–$100, add $10 • $100^{01}–$150, add $12
Over $150, call for shipping charge

Subscriptions   Please ❑ start   ❑ renew my subscription to *New Directions for
Teaching and Learning* for the year _____ at the following rate:

U.S.:	❑ Individual $59	❑ Institutional $114
Canada/Mexico:	❑ Individual $59	❑ Institutional $154
All Others:	❑ Individual $83	❑ Institutional $188

$ _____   Total single issues and subscriptions (Add appropriate sales tax
for your state for single issue orders. No sales tax for U.S. subscriptions.
Canadian residents, add GST for subscriptions and single issues.)

❑ Payment enclosed (U.S. check or money order only)

❑ VISA, MC, AmEx, Discover Card #_____ Exp. date_____

Signature _____ Day phone _____

❑ Bill me (U.S. institutional orders only. Purchase order required)

Purchase order #_____

Federal Tax ID 135593032   GST 89102-8052

Name _____

Address _____

_____

Phone_____ E-mail _____

For more information about Jossey-Bass, visit our Web site at:
www.josseybass.com   **PRIORITY CODE = ND1**